MW00966260

BE THE CHANGE

A Story. A Roadmap. A Movement.

Christy,
Thanks for your love and
support. Keep shining ♡
xox
Marin

MARIN MCCUE

Copyright © 2017 Marin McCue. All rights reserved.
Book Design by Piper Goodfellow
Water colours by Every-Tuesday Teela
ISBN 978-1-387-16476-9

"To be what you must, you must give up what you are."

Yusuf Islam

CONTENTS

Treasure
Reframe Your Story
Vulnerability
Foundation
REPEAT AFTER ME
REFLECT, LEARN, GROW

Programmed by Religion
Mormonism
Fear: What is it Really?
Self-Talk
Mental Models
REPEAT AFTER ME
REFLECT, LEARN, GROW

Basketball
Eating Disorder
Mindful Eating
Growth Mindset vs Fixed Mindset
Recruitment
Happiness Baseline
REPEAT AFTER ME
REFLECT, LEARN, GROW

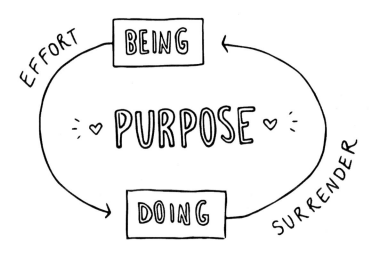

"Real change requires a combination of Being and Doing. Being, which represents the path of the spiritual seeker, stems from ending our inner wars, freeing ourselves from the judgments and limitations of the ego, radiating love, and being the change we wish to see in the world. It's about ending the story of separation and inviting those who participate in the system to make kind, compassionate choices, trusting that real change starts with accepting the world as it is, seeing perfection in it, and then practicing love as an invitation to others to step into their higher selves.

Being without Doing risks keeping love in a theoretical realm, a safe realm where it isn't tested and developed by encounters with the world. Moreover, we are not separate beings. To exist is to relate. Sooner or later, this state of peaceful Being naturally leads to Doing, stemming not from righteousness or moral outrage but from love."

The Anatomy of a Calling by Lissa Rankin

GRATITUDE

    This book is the result of conversations, insights, inquiries and support from many amazing people in my life. I am so grateful for everyone who has played big and small roles in getting this book out into the world. I do not take your time or support for granted. To my friends who graciously read through the first few editions, which were somewhat chaotic: you are rock stars! I am confident in this book's power and impact because of your thoughtful feedback.

    To all of you who contributed to the kickstarter campaign and then reached out to support even after the kickstarter concluded without reaching my goal, you all light me up! Akhila Padmanabahan, Amanda Gill, Angelin Kachor, Andrew Elford, Bruce Dunham, Caitlin Campbell, Cory Tomlinson, Dawn Zentner, David Campagna, Fred and Sue Robertson, Jeff Zanini, Juli James, Katrina Prokopy, Katrina Wilhelm, Lyndi Shaw, Mandy Balak, Natasha Spencer, Ron Schmeichel, Sarah Anderson and Tony Esteves. You all have a special place in my heart.

    To my mama's sister, aunt Terri, your experience and support helped me feel confident even when I realized there's a lot I don't know about the publishing process. You kept me mindful of what questions I need to ask and what to look for. Thank you for being so generous with your time.

    To the wonderful ladies at Parker PR, Ellen Parker and Allison Long, working with you two held me accountable to deadlines and kept me encouraged through the process. You cheered me on and made me feel like anything is possible.

    To my mom, I am continually in awe of your compassion, love, and overall ability to be my mom and my friend. You are my biggest cheerleader and you ask for nothing in return, except connection. I admire your strength and appreciate your vulnerability. Even though you live in France, you somehow make me feel like you are close by. I have not been the kindest and most respectful daughter, and you have never made me feel anything but loved. You accept me and love me no matter what, and I strive to be a better person so that I can be more of what you deserve in our relationship. I know that my confidence and strength comes from the love you give without expectation. Thanks for being my mom and for constantly teaching me what love truly looks like.

Mikael Raheem, my first editor extraordinaire. Your attention to detail and gentle nudges and questions were exactly what I needed during the creation of this book. I am forever grateful for your time and support, and will recommend you to anyone who is in need of editing.

My second editor, Lorraine Valestuk, your excitement and support in this project was exactly what I needed to fine-tune and sculpt this book into its completion. I am in awe of your generosity and inspired by your story. I am so grateful that this project brought you into my life.

And finally, Piper Goodfellow. My graphic designer who brought life to this book by transforming my messy sketches into beautiful images. You created the book cover I had envisioned, spent hours formatting and you did it all with so much passion and excitement. You are amazing! Working with you was the best way to conclude this project. Your creativity and lust for life is a beautiful gift and I am so grateful for you. This book is the piece of art this it is because of you. Thank you for being such a beam of light and for sharing your talents for this project. I love you forever.

How I Suggest You Read This Book

One thing I know for sure: there will be moments in this book that will make you uncomfortable—starting in the preface. My intention is not to sugar coat or shy away from the extreme highs and lows that this life has to offer. So fair warning, get comfortable with being uncomfortable. You may also notice that when you read something that differs from your own current beliefs, you will feel the need to defend or prove me wrong. I am not here to prove anyone wrong or suggest my way of thinking or living is "the way." What I do want is to create a conversation that will offer a wider perspective and deepen your own self-inquiry through questions and curiosity. I am happy to engage with you to further this discourse but not if it comes from a place of anger. Sit with your reactions and breathe through what comes up for you. There is a lesson to be learned every time you feel yourself get triggered.

I encourage anyone reading this book to do so in layers. Read it all the way through in one sitting or take it on chapter by chapter. Then read it in smaller doses and take time to truly reflect and get curious about your own patterns with the support of the "Repeat After Me" and "Reflect, Learn, Grow" portion at the end of each chapter. The Road Map at the end of the book is there to support your integration process as you embark on your own journey with some new tools and inspiration in your repertoire. Allow my words to work like seeds being planted. While I hand you a packet of seeds, it's your job to plant them, nurture them, and enjoy the process of growth. Slow down to speed up. Take time to take notes, underline, and ponder the questions throughout the book. Try opening to random pages and accept whatever message you are ready to receive. Bring it up in conversations, or start a book club. We are creatures of habit, so do yourself a favor and build in repetition and reminders to bring in new energy and new ideas into your mind and body. Change happens when you get off auto-pilot and respond to your environment with the present moment's fresh perspective.

There are a lot of concepts, metaphors, practices, challenges and examples on these pages. I believe it is important, and fun, to introduce a plethora of good vibration ideas and stories, but what I really hope you walk away with is the inspiration to get deeply curious about your own mind, your own story and your own unique way to live as your best self.

Throughout this book, I have included pictures of my art work, as painting was a huge part of my journey through darkness. I share these as examples of my creative process and a reminder that finding your flow activities and creative passions will support your journey as well.

In an attempt to support you along the way, I have gathered key phrases and quotes at the end of each chapter, which I deem to be important to repeat in your inner dialogue, hence the title "Repeat After Me." Again, think of these as seeds to be planted. Repeat them and let them grow roots.

At the end, I propose a road-map that has worked well for me. Use mine to develop the tools you need to create your own best-self pathway. You know what works for you much better than I do, whether you realize that or not. I hope my suggestions will serve as the reminders you need to dive into your own inner-world.

Together we will change the conversation around our mental health struggles into a place of empowerment and understanding. We all have shadows, so let's embrace our darkness and stand taller in your light.

PREFACE

I had never been so lost. I was no stranger to self-loathing but the frantic nature of my feelings had reached a new high. I was dealing with unexplored levels of pain, anger and disgust with myself. The pressure inside of me felt as though it were building without a release valve.

It was an exceptionally hot summer day in Edmonton, one of a couple occurrences just below forty degrees Celsius. I was home alone in my apartment and had been contemplating getting outside all morning to no avail. Instead, I slouched deeper into the couch and continued to make excuses to watch one more mindless TV episode. I had nowhere I needed to be and there was nothing I wanted to accomplish, yet I was overwhelmed with the urge to do something, anything. I knew I would feel better if I went outside or got busy on a project or connected with a friend, but my mind was moving a mile a minute and I couldn't focus on any idea long enough to step outside my erratic and negative bubble.

I was taking a couple of summer classes at the University of Alberta and had convinced my parents that I was incapable of having a job at the same time. I had way too much time on my hands and my normal mental state was toxic with negative self-talk and depression. I felt guilty for taking advantage of my parents' kindness. I felt pathetic. Layer on some crippling fear, direction-less anger, mind-consuming confusion, an overall sense of lack and emptiness, and a spiral downward as I stressed about how much I was stressed. That was the cocktail of emotions I was trying hard to stay afloat in.

My every day was dominated by a cycle of negative self-talk that devolved into self-loathing. At some point each day, this would drive me to tears (or a bucket of ice cream and then tears). Over the last couple of months this vicious cycle had worsened until I found myself in that moment: ready to do something drastic as a way to escape myself.

I aimlessly sauntered to the kitchen and grabbed a serrated steak knife. Without thinking, I started slow, pushing the blade into my left forearm a few inches above where the face of a wrist watch would sit. This briefly directed my drowning mind away from the negative thought-cycle to which I had become victim. I felt a sense of relief as my skin broke and small beads of blood began to form. I finally had a visual for the pain I had been feeling inside.

I knew what I was doing did not make sense but, in that moment, it seemed like my best option. I became transfixed by the blade gripping my skin with its sharp edges, ripping through the first few layers of my arm. I pushed the knife in deeper, making a long horizontal cut. As the blood began to pour, it was like I could breathe for the first time in months. But as quickly as the relief came, it left, leaving more lack and confusion than before. I panicked as blood dripped to the floor.

I cried as I thought about how far I had fallen. I cried for my lost soul. I cried for the fearless girl I once was, the girl who had become buried beneath years of self-criticism. As the pain faded into a dull ache, it was clear that this experiment was a cry for help. I made myself a bandage with paper towel and masking tape, a hideous attempt at self-care without washing or inspecting the severity of my wound. I washed the knife and the floor with much more care than I gave myself. I sat down and stared wide-eyed at the wall. My forearm pulsed ominously. How did I become this person? I thought of myself as a talented and outwardly confident woman, yet I was hiding a darkness that was growing stronger. For a brief moment, it felt like I had found a curb to sit on during my spiral downward but I knew I couldn't sit for long.

When my boyfriend came over that night, I made up a story to explain my wound. I pointed to the door frame where there were a few pieces of jagged wood sticking out and said that I had stumbled due to my notorious absent-mindedness and lack of spatial awareness. He didn't think to question me further.

Two days later, I cut myself again. I craved the feeling of that knife on my skin. The bizarre nature of that feeling started to ring an alarm deep inside me. My anxiety and anger towards myself was the strongest neural pathway in my brain. My dominant wish was to become numb and punish myself for being weak. It only took a couple of slashes to reopen my barely healed wounds. It scared me to notice that I wasn't appalled by my actions. It had come to this. I was intentionally harming myself physically instead of just mentally and emotionally.

This time the story of scraping my arm on the door did not suffice for my partner. I did not want this to become another spiral that grew in severity. I knew I wouldn't last much longer in that case. Although I was embarrassed and ashamed, I needed him to know my secret. I wanted to feel better. I wanted to be better. I wanted to step out of my own dark bubble and be able to contribute to the wellness of others who struggle as I was struggling.

I knew I wanted to change, I just didn't know how.

INTRODUCTION: It's Always Darkest Before the Dawn

"People have a hard time letting go of their suffering. Out of a fear of the unknown, they prefer suffering that is familiar."

Thich Nhat Hanh

I was 23 and a philosophy student at the University of Alberta when I faced the demons in the preface of this book. It wasn't the first time I had been consumed by darkness, as the last ten years leading up to that event had been a series of extreme highs and lows. I had struggled with an eating disorder and depression from the age of 12; however, the underlying dysfunction started much earlier.

At the age of 18 I experienced my first heart-wrenching failure when my dream of being a professional athlete slowly crumbled over the course of a season playing Division 1 college basketball. My inability to bounce-back from that disappointment amplified my pre-existing struggle with mental health. I had worked my whole life on my outer appearance, focused on what others saw and thought of me. I had no idea how to nourish and strengthen my inner self. It took a series of wake-up calls to get me to the realization that my life was headed in a direction that I was not willing to explore much longer.

It was time to educate myself on what was happening in my mind and body and become passionately curious and invested in turning my life around. The surprising gift that came from this journey was a growing passion to coach and inspire others in their own journeys. As I became more vulnerable and open with what I was going through, I found that almost everyone had been through (or was currently going through) something similar, at least in intensity and difficulty. We all have a story. We all have periods of grappling with life's big questions and looming uncertainties.

I discovered that my story and my vulnerability are tools I

can use to connect, empathize and heal. I share my strength, my knowledge, and my creativity, in my own perfectly imperfect way, and in turn, all of these qualities grow deeper roots within myself.

The other day I was leading a few workshops at a local dance studio for teen girls. My task was to teach and inspire them to see the power they have in shifting their self-talk patterns, to understand the relationship between their conscious and subconscious, and how that is the catalyst to positive change in all areas of their life. At the end of a session, one of the girls pulled me aside. With tears beginning to form in her eyes, she looked up at me and asked, "What do you think of anti-depressants?" I responded that I had been on various anti-depressants from the age of 13 to 22, and I think they can be quite beneficial to bring balance into your system. However, it's equally important to learn and practice new skills to cope and grow so that there is a possibility for the medication to be either decreased or removed from the equation eventually. She nodded her head in agreement and then shared that she has been on several anti-depressants for over two years now, which means—in her words—"I am now considered to be mentally ill." This broke my heart. The way she spoke those words accompanied by the bewildered look of defeat on her face took me back to my own struggles growing up.

My response: "Hon, we are *all* mentally ill."

We all struggle. We all go through phases and stages of development that bring us face to face with our shadows and hypocrisies. We all have moments, days or years where we flounder and question everything. Yes, some more than others. Yes, some of us rise above these challenges at a quicker rate. And yes, some lucky few had the right conditions present in their mind, body and environment that allowed them to barely struggle with mental health issues at all. But even those people at least know someone who is deep in a struggle. We are all affected.

We can all agree that the WHY in understanding your mind is obvious: know your machine so you can better navigate through life. It's the HOW that we get tripped up on. What I have discovered through my own experience and through copious amounts of reading and conversations is that we need a simple structure to follow and a deep understanding of how to be disciplined in order to create change within ourselves. This is what so many of us are searching for. We know we want to change, we know there is a better way, we know something is missing, but WHAT is it that we really want, and HOW do we make this "want" a reality?

I believe that when we share our shadows and lessons learned with an inquisitive mind and a passion for growth, we leave bread crumbs for ourselves and others to find and sustain the course of self-development. We are all capable of moments of greatness, and when we learn to conserve and create more quality energy we can tap into our greatness more and more. That's the overarching goal of this book: *to teach, guide and inspire you to see how you can create and conserve more quality fuel for your journey.*

Here are some facts to consider—keep in mind these are an average and will look slightly different for each person on a day-to-day basis:

> More than 40% of actions taken each day are habitual (Duhigg 2012).
> Your subconscious mind is at the helm approximately 95% of your day. And up to 95% of what you think today, you also thought yesterday (Duhigg 2012).
> 65-77% of what the average person thinks on a daily basis is negative or self-defeating (Helmstetter 1986).
> 40% of what you "see" comes in through your eyes, the rest is filled in with assumptions, experience, perception, memory, expectations and beliefs (Lipton 2005).
> The Sympathetic Nervous System is triggered into fight or flight response 50 - 300 times per day (Rankin 2016).

When I think about these statistics and notice the common

struggles we all share, I see an opportunity for a huge shift within our world. If we could support each other into a place of self-love and develop a deeper understanding of how and why we think what we think and act how we act, we could create a generation of mindful, healthy and creative thinkers. Ultimately, if you want to see change in the world, change in your relationships, change in your habits, and ultimately, change in your perspective of life and happiness, it starts with your thoughts.

I am now 31 and look back on my life with gratitude. For years I lived life as a prisoner in my own mind and body, and now I have a mindset that I did not believe would ever be possible for me. I make a modest living doing what I love and I use my story to inspire and motivate others to take charge of the change they want to see in their life.

I know everyone learns differently. I went to several therapists and was prescribed several medications, but the change I wanted in my life did not set in until I became invested and in charge of my own development through reading and writing. I read dozens upon dozens of books, and have had many more inspiring conversations that challenged, provoked and cracked me open to new ways of being and doing. My glimmering goal behind this project is fueled by the idea that someone can pick up this book, when the timing is right, and have it be the catalyst to positive change in their life. Whether you are reading these words in an attempt for support or are simply intrigued by a good story, take some time to reflect and practice the concepts that stand out to you as you read. We can all learn and grow by being open to the words of another.

"It is good to have an end to journey toward, but it is the journey that matters in the end"

Ursula Le Guin

~

CHAPTER 1: Hero's Journey

"A hero ventures forth from the world of common day into a region of supernatural wonder: fabulous forces are there encountered and a decisive victory is won: the hero comes back from this mysterious adventure with the power to bestow boons on his fellow man."

The Hero with a Thousand Faces by Joseph Campbell

Author Joseph Campbell identified a sequence of events shared within most narratives, myths and real life renditions of the human condition. He explained this as a monomyth, or a "Hero's Journey," and this insight has been rehashed by countless people since its appearance in Campbell's 1949 book *The Hero with a Thousand Faces*.

What we see continually through historical stories is a series of events in pivotal steps that create adventure and growth opportunities for the main character. But it is important to consider, the nature of being human brings with it many varieties and unique situations. Although the Hero's Journey is typically depicted in a certain order, when I reflect on my life, I see cycles, missteps, successes, growth, discovery, loss, support, darkness, light, energy... I could go on. It may feel good to organize, label and clean up the edges to make everything appear like it fits exactly where it was supposed to go, but just because our brain likes order, that doesn't mean life comes at you that way. As we all know, hindsight is 20/20. Telling a story is a whole lot cleaner than living it. While you may relate to some parts of my story, yours is unique and carries different complexities. From a big picture perspective, we are all a part of the same unifying story, but it is vital to honor our own experience and witness our own capabilities within the community at large.

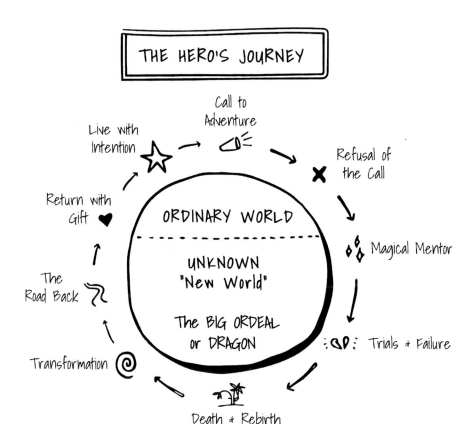

THE HERO'S JOURNEY

Call to Adventure

Live with Intention

Refusal of the Call

Return with Gift ♥

ORDINARY WORLD

UNKNOWN "New World"

Magical Mentor

The Road Back

The BIG ORDEAL or DRAGON

Trials + Failure

Transformation ◎

Death + Rebirth

What do you need to know about the Hero's Journey? The character begins in an ordinary world, with a sense of emptiness and an inkling that there is much more to life than what they have been exposed to. From there, our character contemplates adventure when an opportunity arises, but they need the assistance and wisdom of a magical mentor to gain the courage to take the leap. This will be one of many magical mentors in our Hero's life, as collaborating in mutually supportive relationships proves to be vital. Our Hero moves forward through highs and lows, trials and failures, roadblocks and setbacks, and lessons learned as fear and self-doubt begin to loosen their grip. Through meeting allies and enemies and learning the new rules of this world, the journey unfolds. Down the road, our Hero faces their "dragon," their "big ordeal" or rock-bottom. By no means is this battle short-lived (this is where living the journey truly becomes messy compared to narrating the story).

In defeating this darkness our Hero uncovers a new found confidence, develops new skills and discovers a treasure far beyond their wildest expectations. Life being the bumpy road that it is, nothing comes easily. There are few moments of calm and assurance until our Hero makes the journey back into the ordinary world, resembling who they once were yet far different on the inside. Through loss and rebirth, the threshold between these two worlds are bridged. Like a phoenix from the ashes the old self is burned away and the new self emerges with treasure in hand.

Treasure

But what is this treasure?
Through centuries of lives come and gone, we have witnessed and heard stories of the shared human condition to pursue a life of meaning. We have learned to see treasure in enlightenment and wisdom. We know that treasures are found in unexpected and often dark and protected places. The treasure found at the end of a Hero's Journey is something that was within you all along. It is hidden by routine, fears and compulsions that we habitually shame ourselves for or run from. Through the act of learning to face yourself, to see your hypocrisies, swim in your darkness and to meet the feelings that make you the most uncomfortable, you can come into contact with this innate treasure.

Have I found my treasure? I am fascinated with the process of evolving into a more conscious, balanced, and happy being. This passion has opened me up to vast experiences that I am privileged to have participated in. These experiences have gifted me with the tools and creative power to support and elevate as many people around me as I can. The true nature of my treasure will become clearer as you read on.

Reframe your Story

Many of us have to learn the same lesson several times before it actually leaves a lasting impression. What I have found in my own life and through the storytelling of others is that without conscious and deliberate re-framing of our own story, there are likely to be dark corners of our mind and times in our life that we avoid or keep to ourselves out of shame or confusion. These raw wounds and undigested experiences that we deliberately avoid end up being the foundation of our own limiting beliefs, assumptions, and patterns that disrupt our progress and growth. These are the chapters in our life where we were victims or abusers, where we failed to show up or we chose the non-hero path despite "knowing better." It is in our shame and the painful emotions of recalling our story that we create an armored heart with fear and anxiety guarding the walls.

Imagine the possibility of re-framing what you believe and relearning what you are capable of. Imagine how powerful you could feel if you welcomed each moment into your heart with open arms and an open mind. Imagine being ready to receive the gifts of every new opportunity without being jaded by past experiences or a fabricated idea of what the future holds. Some of your current beliefs or expectations are healthy and empowering, but I am sure you can pinpoint a few that make you feel inadequate, stuck, incapable or lethargic. It is in the low-energy, low-vibration, limiting beliefs and habits that the Hero's Journey can support you to uncover and replace.

Reframing your story is a fascinating process but it is also a challenge to meet head on. The process can be quite uncomfortable at first, but the journey and the results are worth it. Your positive experiences will be profound and nourishing while the heaviness of your dark moments will evoke greater learning opportunities. This will give you capacity to bounce back at a much quicker pace.

It is important to note that a practice of contentment and gratitude will be vital to keep high quality fuel in your system. We need the daily reminder that each passing moment is perfectly imperfect, and it is what it is. Contentment opens you up to all ranges of emotions. It is our resistance and avoidance of "what is" that creates the lasting struggle. When you wholeheartedly open yourself to the moment at hand and allow yourself to feel whatever is coming up for you, it will pass through you and leave you ready for the next moment. This is where your higher Self is patiently waiting to be engaged.

To be discontent is to fall for the illusion that there can be something else in this moment other than what is. That doesn't mean the next moment will be the same. In fact, while you accept and love this moment for what it is, you are setting the foundation for growth that could create a shift in perspective for the next moment. There are always things to learn and there will be future opportunities where you can show up differently if you choose, but this moment is what it is. Allow yourself to be at ease with boredom, be content with sadness, and embrace loss and depression with peace. What you resist, persists. As Deborah Adele says: "Being content with our discontentment is itself a gateway to the calm depths within" (*The Yamas and Niyamas*, 2009).

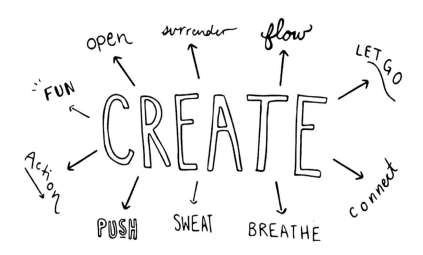

Try using this mind-map format when you have a word you want to focus on at a deeper level, or understand or visualize what it feels like or looks like in action.

To truly create and conserve quality energy, we must look at ways we are needlessly draining our own energy. We all have biological impulses that prime us to judge, compare, assume, expect, desire, and fear. The key is to develop the ability to spend time understanding these impulses while encouraging more focus on growth, flow, learning, curiosity, trust, and love. Because where your mind goes, energy flows.

Foundation

One of my favorite reminders is to refer to our innermost beliefs, habits and core values as the foundation beneath our feet from which we stand and grow. These beliefs, habits, and core values are what fuels, nourishes, guides and comforts us. However, they can also be what drains, depletes, isolates, and paralyzes us. If you are unclear in what you believe, what your habits are and how they are serving you, or how your core values can support your decision-making, then you are not taking full advantage of your unique potential. When there is a crack in the foundation or a disconnection between you and your foundation, you will find yourself in a less than ideal situation and realize you don't have the support or stability to handle anything other than calm and mild weather. And life is anything but calm and mild.

It is in our ability to get curious and question our beliefs about life, love, success, relationships and growth, that allows us to uncover where we are actually holding ourselves back. When we discover our own limiting beliefs that have been subconsciously ruling our thoughts and behaviour, it can feel like the ground being ripped from under you as you realize the foundation you have been standing on for years was just an illusion, a self-created existence pieced together and bought into. A foundation full of cracks cannot sustain the new growth you desire in life.

To begin this process of retraining your brain to create new healthy habits, a simple commitment of ten minutes a day is all it takes. I spent at least ten minutes each day, for one year, thinking about this book or certain sections I was stuck on, in conversation with others, drawing out images and diagrams, or simply letting my thoughts flow into the words you are reading now. I knew this was a marathon not a sprint and my subconscious mind would stay motivated if I made the daily goal realistic and attainable. Sustainable growth is a commitment to small steps with persistence.

When we make continual huge efforts, we lose steam—ultimately, we make it a lot harder than it needs to be. We need to make minor adjustments on our course and practice living in the moment so we can enjoy this precious and volatile existence while we have it.

When you are able to tap into the power of observing your thought patterns, you can begin to edit as you notice where you lose power and where you gain power. To truly know yourself and find what your purpose in this life can be, I suggest you commit to one year of writing your memoir within the blueprint of the Hero's Journey.

In the book *Living Your Yoga*, Judith Lasater refers to our many layers and our self-discovery by saying,

"When carving stone, the sculptor removes everything that is not the statue. She does not add anything to create it, except the willingness to do the work. The art of revealing beauty lies in removing what conceals it."

Vulnerability

When I think of vulnerability I feel a warm sensation wash over my mind and body. To be vulnerable is to show up as everything that you are, your raw self with nothing to hide, while embracing your perfectly imperfect human ways. For many, vulnerability seems scary and dangerous at first, and I have found that this is generally due to a fear of being judged. I enjoy being open and vulnerable with my current states. I notice that when I do so, others begin to open up and share more of what is true for them in that moment. Part of the practice of vulnerability involves over-sharing—with good intentions—only to realize that too much of a good thing is not a good thing. We can go to the extreme in absolutely anything we do, and even with a beautiful gift like "vulnerability," moderation and mindfulness guides us to share from a place of empowerment and desire for growth rather than dumping our undigested emotions and thoughts onto the lap of another. But we don't find our edges or grow our strength and abilities without occasionally pushing outside our comfort zone and overstepping boundaries. We learn by doing.

I still get vulnerability hangovers after sharing a lot of myself or when I make bold moves without knowing how they will land. But, in the end, it takes less energy to be authentic and vulnerable than it does to be a people-pleaser, a mask-wearer, or to worry and second-guess your actions. Vulnerability is the willingness to show up and be seen without any assurances that you will have a soft spot to land when or if you fall. But it is when we fall that we gain the most, as I can see now as I reflect on where I have been. Vulnerability is less about you and more about the openness and inclusivity you invite into the space. It is contagious. It creates empathy and connection with anyone who is open and receptive to your real-ness (which won't be everyone).

The fear we feel when approaching vulnerability is best remedied by facing it head on. We can get used to almost anything, for better or for worse, so I suggest the practice of not being held back by fears that are nothing more than your over-protective mind and wild imagination.

Openly sharing my inner self with others did not come easily at first. I was in the habit of keeping things hidden, showing only what I thought people wanted or what made me feel good. I have learned that, although I love to be a lone-wolf in many aspects of my life, true vulnerability and courage is found in authentic connection with others. I am not doing anyone any good when I pretend I am someone other than who I am or create the appearance that life has been easy. I am not teaching or inspiring from a place of authentic realness if I sugar-coat my experiences or keep my important lived lessons to myself. Life can be really dark, heavy, overwhelming and, for many, it can become too much to bare. When we open up to these sorts of conversations we begin to create a safe place for others to share and to realize that they are not alone in their struggles.

I am not here to proclaim that I am a Hero or that my story is any more tantalizing or tragic than anyone else's. We all have a story and we all get to be the Hero of our own narrative. When you acknowledge that your story is the inspiration and foundation beneath your feet and not the weight on your back, you will find your strength, build your resilience, and witness your capacity to gracefully handle whatever life throws your way.

If my vulnerability in re-telling and re-framing my life's events helps you view your toughest moments as something to own proudly and learn from, then my mission has been accomplished.
I hope to have many more years to experience and add depth with new chapters to my journey. But for now, this is it. Welcome to my Hero's Journey.

For more inspiration and conversation around vulnerability, check out Brene Brown's books or TED Talks.

"What we are today comes from our thoughts of yesterday, and our present thoughts build our life of tomorrow: Our life is the creation of our mind."

Buddha

~

(REPEAT AFTER ME)

The treasure found at the end of a Hero's Journey is something that was within you all along. It is hidden by the habits, fears, and compulsions that we habitually shame ourselves for or run from.

— • —

Without conscious and deliberate re-framing of our own story, there are likely to be dark corners of our mind and times in our life that we avoid or keep to ourselves out of shame or confusion.

— • —

Where your mind goes, energy flows.

— • —

We all have a story and we all get to be the Hero of our own narrative once we learn to own our story as the inspiring foundation beneath our feet versus the weight on our back.

— • —

It takes less energy to be authentic and vulnerable than it does to be a people-pleaser, a mask-wearer, or to worry and second-guess your actions.

— • —

Vulnerability is less about you and more about the openness and inclusivity you invite into the space.

Reflect, LEARN, GROW

1. Where are you on your Hero's Journey?

2. Have you found your "treasure"? What do you think it is?

3. How has the term "vulnerability" been used in your life? Does it carry a negative connotation?

4. Write out a description of "vulnerability" used in a positive light:

5. How do you understand the importance and integral role of vulnerability now?

CHAPTER 2: Ordinary World

"What we know from past experience is an asset, but what leads to successful transformation is our capacity to learn in real time. While knowledge is useful, learning is essential."

Building the Bridge as You Walk on it by Robert E. Quinn

Last family photo before my parent's divorce (2008) — From top left to right: Brayden, Kieran, Dallin, Mom, Dad, Carl (Katie's husband), Katie (holding her first born, Darius — three more have arrived since then), Amanda, Ayden (Amanda's son), Teresa, and me, crawling (*I know*).

I was a tough little girl, with a sweet innocent smile and a giggle that could win over any audience. Beneath that smile, I was a conniving little rapscallion. I was curious, vivacious, and pushed boundaries just to test the limits. I don't think I was a pure deviant child by any means—I had my moments of compassion and moderation—but I preferred the rush of living in the extremes of sugar highs and adrenaline rushes. I was simply an inexperienced human with little supervision and three older siblings that I loved to entertain. I was unaware of how my actions could hurt others and not too concerned with anyone's feelings but my own.

I was born into a Mormon family in 1986 in Vancouver, British Columbia. As the middle child of seven kids with a mother and father who started a family when they were barely in their twenties, it didn't take me long to notice the stress and exhaustion my parents lived with. Without a strong bond, other than church-imposed ceremonies and expectations, my parents did not make each other happy, and I often wished they would get a divorce.

Programmed by Religion

Despite being skeptical of the church from an early age, it was all I knew. Before I was eight years old I had been exposed to a couple thousand hours of conditioning through ceremonies, television broadcasts, movies, classrooms, group activities, and lessons on The Book of Mormon. It was a part of who I was and how I viewed life. My perception of life was molded from the limited perspective and boundaries of religion. I would ask questions to understand death, how to interpret or understand the validity of our scriptures, and how other religions could be all wrong while we were the only "true" church, but I was hushed and told to pray for my answers and, ultimately, to just believe. I did pray, every day.

Sometimes my prayers were routine and spouted out without much conscious effort. Other times I prayed with eagerness and intensity as I tried to converse with my image of God. Although I never felt connected or heard a response to my prayers, it did not stop me from trying. For example, when I was 14, I prayed and pleaded several times asking for a sex dream. My logic, as I explained in my prayer, was that this would help me avoid real-life sexual contact with boys (pre-marital sex is a big no-no in that culture). If I knew I could experience this tantalizing and exciting urge in my dreams, I then could avoid this premarital "sin." Sadly, my prayers weren't answered.

I never noticed or felt anything that I could quantify as a response during or after any of my prayers. The one aspect of the church that I felt made it special was the collective experience of the community. Leaders and faithful followers in the church would often describe an overwhelming feeling of being swept away by a higher power and would equate this to the Spirit of God or the Holy Ghost[1] guiding them. This feeling of a higher power would often be evoked throughout the congregation after a beautiful song, a heartfelt story, or an emotional testimony of faith by a member. I had felt that beautiful feeling. It felt like connection with one and all, while transcending the mundane of the individual. It made me feel like there was something more out there in the universe, but whether that was the space where God resided, I was not sure. All I knew was that there was something much bigger than me and my direct experience with reality. I remember the first time I heard the song "Bittersweet Symphony" by The Verve when I was 16 years old. I was driving alone with my windows down and the music blasting and I was struck with that same overwhelming and magical feeling I had experienced in the church setting. Either the spirit resides in The Verve or I had been misled to believe that feeling was something that it's not. I leaned towards the latter explanation.

Mormonism

To not believe or to express skepticism about wholehearted, blind faith, would create a stir within the family unit and the church: news travels fast when the community is tight-knit and full of account-ability and mentoring hierarchies. The whole family feels guilt and shame when one sibling or parent is known for making "immoral" choices or not actively believing the gospel. Life was a series of rules to follow with blind faith in a system run by fallible people, and I felt I was missing out on a certain amount of creativity, growth and a flow to life.

My dad left the Church when I was 16 and made some big waves within the community—and our family—through the process. He had been a well-known leader in the church for most of his life

---

1   In Mormon culture, the Holy Ghost is the third member of the Godhead (along with God and Jesus). This spirit is considered to be a guiding force of good, keeping members safe and comforted.

and, being the smart and outspoken man that he is, he did not leave the confines of the religion quietly. He started a website to share his questions, his discoveries, and his journey, which served as his therapy during his transition. He continues to get emails from people around the world, some thanking him for providing the knowledge and courage they needed to also leave the church, and others threatening or cursing him for being the "Anti-Christ" of this generation[2].

Perspective is a funny thing. Despite my aversion to the Mormon culture, it does have many great values as well—very few things are all bad or all good. I appreciated the supportive and loving community and the emphasis on the importance of family. There is enough good in the church that many smart and open-minded people stay in the community despite their understanding of where the culture falls short. To each their own. I don't want to create the impression that Mormons are bad people or that I am better than anyone who has stayed within the church. I am simply relaying my experience, and I recognize that this won't speak true to others' experiences. The more self-study and research I engage in, the more I realize that comparisons and making others feel wrong to make me feel "more right" is a pointless game. I know what works for me and what my temperament and belief system lean towards as my true north, and it just did not find that alignment within organized religion.

I knew I was not a bad person, but because I asked a lot of questions and pushed against the rules, I felt a lot of shame, guilt and an underlying sense that something was wrong with me. Despite my scepticism about the validity of the church—and all religions in general—I was still bothered by these feelings of not being "enough" and began to ingrain a self-talk habit of self-doubt and self-loathing.

As a Mormon, at age eight we are baptised as consenting individuals who choose to receive the Holy Ghost as well as the responsibility of paying tithing and repenting for sins from that day on. Tithing is an expectation for members to "donate" to the church

---

2   He has also written some great articles with information on what the process of basketball recruitment looked like and what we wish we knew while we were going through it ourselves. You can find his writing at www.bobmccue.ca.

ten percent of all money made, every month. As an eight-year-old I thought this was crazy. I knew that any money I would get my hands on for the next few years was coming from my parents or from other Mormon couples who I babysat for, which meant that money had already been through the process of being tithed. It didn't make sense to me that I would need to pay that ten percent again. I tried to barter with the Bishop. I explained my point of view with the aim to get my tithing commitment down to five percent. Of course, my negotiations did not succeed, and in the end the Bishop pulled my dad aside and warned him that he may need to keep a close eye on me. Dad nodded as he was already fully aware.

Dad and I had a few altercations weekly as he was overworked and paying his way through law school, supporting a growing family and a chronically depressed wife, and holding high positions in the church. We have a much healthier and balanced relationship now. But when I was young I often would dread the sound of his car rolling into the garage because I had already been promised a spank upon his arrival due to my misbehaving during the day.

One consistent point of conflict was from my dad's house rule that we must wear socks at all times. My dad had been raised to believe that wearing socks indoors was a must. Something about the oils or dirt on the feet that could ruin the carpet quicker. He laughs at the notion now but when you are overworked and struggling to keep a growing family afloat, the default rules and beliefs you grew up with take over. It's amazing how lack of sleep and loads of stress can turn off our reasoning capabilities.

He saw it as a sign of disrespect and disregard for rules when he would catch any of us barefoot in the house. On several occasions, we would hear dad's car pulling into the driveway late at night and everyone would run looking for socks to put on. I was the youngest at the time and often could not find socks so instead I would wrap a blanket around my lower body. This never fooled dad. I tease him now, but it seemed like we had a routine weekly spanking appointment through my early years.

I don't remember being halted by fear often when I was little, but an angry look from my dad? That put the fear of God in me. I climbed big trees and fell out of big trees. I ran and played with my older siblings and their friends. I crashed my bike flying down hills that I had no business riding, got into fights—mostly verbal jousting but I occasionally put my fists up ready to rumble—and suffered at least one major concussion from being a cocky and over-confident five-year-old playing red-rover with the older kids in our cul-de-sac.

When I hit puberty at around 12 years old, my fear patterns changed drastically. I went from confident and self-assured to being stumped by fear at every turn and obsessively focused on what others thought of me. Because of this drastic transition, I became transfixed by fear and—once I was an adult—needed to understand the grip it had on me. As I have done with any concept I am curious about, I start with gaining an understanding of the purpose and etymology of the term.

Fear: What is it Really?

Like all emotions, fear is energy coursing down a neural pathway. It is a signal from our overprotective subconscious system which communicates (with chemicals rather than words) that something unknown or dangerous is up ahead. Either our experience is reminding us of something we have experienced as dangerous or the unknown factors in the situation are perceived as potential for danger. When we feel the grip of fear, it pulls our attention away from anything else happening. From an evolutionary perspective, we have survived because our overactive "fight or flight" response (sympathetic nervous system) grabs our attention with a spurt of the steroid hormone cortisol anytime we perceive (i.e., feel, smell, see, assume, expect, or catastrophize) potential threats to our safety. This goes to show that our subconscious is not connected to reality, but rather is highly influenced by your unique experience and what thoughts you allow into your mind. What I find most fascinating about cortisol is that generally when we feel its buzz it is because we are thinking about something in the past or projecting ourselves into the possibilities of the future. When you are actually in physical danger, there's often not time to even think about the danger before you are forced to react to it. In our day and age we are flooded with cortisol habitually and unnecessarily.

Cortisol gives us that "do something" feeling, along with a burst of energy to run, fight or freeze. This remarkable system kept our ancestors alive and continues to keep us fortunate evolution winners alive to this day. The chemical cortisol has gotten somewhat of a bad reputation because of our overly stressed, controlling, anxious and fearful ways of living. But in small doses, cortisol is healthy and necessary. We need a bit of stress, and in fact, a bit of trauma is actually good for us, as it builds resiliency and gratitude for the precious nature of life and its many gifts.

What I find most interesting about fear (and stress) is that our perception of these natural reactions will influence the effects they have on our system. The way you think and relate to something will affect how you remember it, how you feel about it, how you show up and what actions you take. The goal is not to get rid of stress or fear, rather, it's to change your relationship with it. For example, those who believe stress is bad for them will actually experience more negative effects than those who believe stress is okay and potentially beneficial. Change the way you perceive stress and fear and you build up your body's ability to respond pragmatically and recover efficiently (Rankin 2015).

As Michael Singer points out in *The Untethered Soul,* "Eventually you will see that the real cause of problems is not life itself. It's the commotion the mind makes about life that really causes problems" (2007).

Instead of asking "How do we become fearless?" we should be asking "How do we change our relationship with fear so we can deal with life's peaks and valleys in a more balanced and healthy way? How can we lean into fear, embrace our struggles, celebrate our challenges, and come out the other side stronger, more resilient, and braver to handle the next storm?"

No matter how well we meet our needs, our brain will be on the lookout for danger. This subconscious mechanism is a beautiful and necessary aspect of our evolution. Thank yourself when you feel fear, and then decide consciously what you will do next because, otherwise, your autopilot will steer you down the same path over and over.

One thing that has helped me immensely is to think about courage as a muscle to flex. The more I practice courage by pushing outside my comfort zone and stepping up to the plate despite my nerves, the easier and easier it becomes.

The fact of the matter is that when we are honest about what we desire and what we want to create in our lives, fear will come along for the ride and will most likely ride shotgun. We fear that we will not get what we want. We fear that we will be rejected. We fear that we are not worthy of the big and powerful goals we declare. It seems, at first, that we can't win. It's as though being vulnerable and making our bold affirmation of the life we desire is ultimately setting ourselves up for disappointment.

Fear itself is not going to change but your response can. First, acknowledge fear for what it really is: an emotional reaction and energy coursing down a paved neural superhighway of least resistance. Remember that your body and mind are overprotective and are signalling that there is uncertainty in the mix or that you have experienced something similar in your past that did not produce an outcome you loved. But today is a new day and you don't have to allow fear to be the backseat driver it strives to be.

To overcome the habit of allowing fear to create resistance and stagnancy, we must practice feeling the fear and doing it anyway. In *The Untethered Soul, Singer* says "[y]ou will get to a point in your growth where you understand that if you protect yourself, you will never be free, you will not grow."

When I feel the buzz of cortisol or the negative self-talk that pops up reminding me of all the possible ways things can go wrong,

I consciously shift my awareness to focus on the bigger picture. Otherwise, the spiral down takes over, and once the momentum down begins, it takes more energy to shift back up.

So what do I do? I remind myself that nothing lasts forever. I remind myself that I have done tougher things before and I consistently realize that things are not as hard as I make them out to be in my mind. And if that doesn't do the job, I shift my focus onto things that inspire me. I think about what I am creating in my life by making this bold move. I reflect on what I am grateful for and how far I have come. I tell myself what I need to hear. This practice of slowing myself down and choosing the thoughts I want to ruminate over has had a huge impact on my life. Fear may be along for the ride, but it is now in the trunk rather than the driver's seat. It's still there, but it is not the loudest presence. I have filled my metaphorical car with inspiration and reminders to keep me balanced and grounded as I make bold and brave moves in my life. New neural pathways are created by directing energy to courage, playing big, trusting life, and trusting the ability to adapt, evolve and recover. Courage can become the new path of least resistance—but only with daily conscious repetition.

Self-Talk

I wish I had understood more about how to calm the "commotion" in my mind when I was younger. To know how your mind and body connect and to understand how to redirect energy away from negative self-talk loops is an invaluable skill to learn. Whatever we focus on, we create more of. Wherever you focus your attention, you build new or stronger neural connections simply by shining light on whatever you are experiencing. As my all-time favourite mantra sings: where your mind goes, energy flows. The words we use create a ripple effect within ourselves, as well as the environment around us. When we narrate each passing moment, when we communicate our story to others and to ourselves, when we assign meaning to our experiences and when we reflect on our past or project into the future, the words we use carry incredible power in how they make us feel about ourselves and what subsequent actions we take. Your inner dialogue creates the neurochemical soup that your mind and body steep in. What kind of soup have you allowed yourself to soak in today?

In a conversation with my brother recently regarding the power of the words we choose to use, he mentioned a reiki master he studied under in Australia. He said that the words we choose to use put a spell on those who hear it, including ourselves; why else would they call it "spell"-ing? As silly as this first sounds, the more we talked about it the more this blew me away. When we think of our words as actually putting a spell on the ears that they land on, suddenly there is more reason to think about what kind of spell you want to cast.

As I mentioned in the introduction, author Shad Helmstetter, in his book *What to Say When You Talk to Yourself*, states that up to 77% of the average person's thoughts are negative. This makes sense when you factor in that our self-protective subconscious mind is inherently the first to react. We know that our fight-or-flight response is activated 50-300 times per day, on average. This response furthers the feeling that we are unsafe, we don't belong, we are out of alignment with our values, or we don't matter. Our conscious mind reacts to these signals by matching the vibration of what we are feeling with words that add meaning. The result: a large portion of our thoughts can perpetuate unnecessary negative energy.

According to the National Science Foundation, the average person thinks 12,000-50,000 thoughts per day (depending on how deep of a thinker you are) (Kaiser, 2012). This means, on average, we create approximately 9,240 to 38,500 negative thoughts in just one day. No wonder we have an epidemic of depression, anxiety, obesity, and an overall lack of enthusiasm for positivity! Our work is in building the strength of our positive mind to veto the instinct of the negative mind. As is the case with most change challenges, we can land on the "why" and we can see where we want to go, but it is the "how" that stumps us.

Think back to the last time you had a big problem in your life.

What happened? What stories, assumptions, fears, and worries did you sit in during and after? What was worse: "what happened" or the mind-chatter that preceded it? In my experience, my mind-chatter makes things a whole lot worse and wastes precious energy that I would love to invest elsewhere. Don't get me wrong: it is important to reflect and learn from situations, but how can you reflect and learn while being consumed by victim-hood, doom and gloom, or avoiding the situation altogether?

It's not easy, but right from the moment we are traumatically pushed out of our mother's womb, we live with struggles and face disappointment. That is the nature of being the emotional machines that we are. Denying the nature of existence doesn't protect you; it diminishes your light and your power. Imagine the scenario of being face to face with a problem: something that scares you and brings a lot of uncertainty to the table. Now imagine standing tall in the face of this problem and acknowledging its destructive power without being swept up by the many possible outcomes. What if you noticed your reaction and observed the consequent negative self-talk as simply a part of your biology? What if you stopped sending energy down the pathway to negativity the moment you noticed it? What if you saw your power and control in your ability to witness your impulses, reactions and compulsions, and the choice to respond with words and actions that are aligned with who you are, or are striving to be?

Now take a few deep belly breaths to ground yourself and decide what the best first step is to handle and grow through this situation. Is it to reach out to someone you love and admire who will be there to support you? Is it best to write a list of to-dos? Or maybe could you go for a workout and see what creative juices begin to flow? None of these actions are diminishing the gravity of the situation. It is what it is, so what you choose to do, after your reaction, will either elevate you to a place to deal with it or pull you down with weight and darkness that keeps your vision small. When you know how your mind and body work it becomes much easier to coach yourself out of stagnancy and fear and into trust and growth. From low vibration to high vibration. From lack to possibility. From struggle to strength.

So what do I do? I know my mind goes to doom and gloom scenarios first so I thank my mind for being so protective and I'll focus on my breath as I breathe out the energy that I know is not helpful and breathe in energy I need more of. I know my mind works best after a good sweat, so I get my body moving, and I often realize I was being too serious or too caught up in that moment to make a pragmatic decision. I know that when I reach out to others who elevate and love me (and who love themselves wholeheartedly), I will get an impartial perspective and a strong shoulder to cry on if needed. I am not any smarter or better-equipped for stress, but I have built up my ability to find a moment to pause when I feel stressed or triggered, so that I can script my way through it. I trust the process and choose to remind myself that everything is a learning opportunity, everything is an offer, and everything is practice for the next moment. I let myself feel what comes up in each moment, without resistance or anger, I love myself up and slowly release the hurt or scared feelings that surfaced. And if that doesn't work to calm me down, then I remind myself: "it's okay to not feel okay," and suddenly a feeling of acceptance and allowance washes over me. We aren't meant to feel great all the time; sometimes we need to give ourselves permission to just be in our struggle.

Mental Models

A phrase that stuck with me for years while I was re-building the foundation of how I experience life was: "don't believe everything that you think." This reminder served my ability to build awareness in my thoughts and actions and to step back and question where my mind was going rather than feeling like a victim to my own patterns. I discovered that we each have a unique perception of reality that stems from our senses, and this plays a role in creating various perspectives through habitual interpretations and conscious deliberation. The combination of perception and perspective creates the unique mental model—or lens—that you experience as your reality.

Our words have the ability to talk people off the edge or

talk them to their edge. Our words create a reality that can evoke a blueprint for how to engage in life. This blueprint can be many things. It can be dark and full of doom-and-gloom, it can be limiting and deflating, it can be expansive and motivating, it can be complex and full of possibility, it can be simple, and it can be seen as a working metaphor. These are "mental models"[3] and they are passed down through generations or self-created (subconsciously and consciously) based on experience and habit.

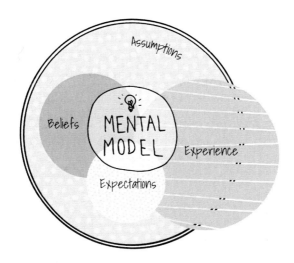

Your "Mental Model" or lens is your unique perspective that is created from your beliefs, assumptions, expectations and meaning derived from experience. Anytime I am feeling stuck, down, or limited by my perspective, I am reminded that there is always a way to shift my "Mental Model" to see things in a new light.

What I love about the contemplation on mental models is the reminder that just because I perceive and experience something a certain way, does not mean that that is the only way or the totality of the situation. Absolutely every thought, emotion, insight, idea, or belief is available to me in each passing moment, but what I perceive is a unique compilation and integration of my inner environment, past experience, beliefs, and expectations. Think back to the last time you were at the optometrist, as you sit in the big comfy chair with the huge

---

3   I first came across this term in the book Creativity, Inc. by Ed Catmull. These are approximations of reality that play a major role in feelings and behaviour. Dating as far back as 1943, Kenneth Craik wrote about our mind's ability to construct "small-scale models" of reality to anticipate and navigate events.

contraption pulled in front of your face. Lens after lens being dropped in front of your eyes to test your vision. "Is one better or maybe number two? Now, is this third one more clear or maybe number four? Now, try this one or would you say back to this previous one?" As each new lens is added or taken away your vision becomes blurrier or sharper until you land on the combination that suits your unique vision. Now imagine each lens is a different belief about life, different expectations and assumptions about success, and new ideas and new experiences that expand your mind and broaden your understanding of what's possible. Your mental model may feel like absolute truth, and may have served you well, but when you can practice being aware of the subjectivity in your mental models and the opportunity for growth and releasing that which does not serve you well, suddenly life becomes a little more intriguing.

For example, one person could view balance as a triangle: the foundation being the long edge at the base with what they deem to be grounding priorities of life, while the point at the top represents the occasional need to be pushed outside their comfort zone. Another person could view balance as an inverted triangle: the base being the point of the triangle which represents being grounded in who they are at the core, while the long base at the top represents the many priorities and roles this person plays in life. And another person could view balance as a dance; a constant expansion and contraction that moves and shifts, expresses out to experience newness and comes back to the centre for grounding and stability; a moving target that is felt and experienced with each mindful breath rather than seen or drawn in a diagram. The words we use to understand key concepts and motivate action differs from person to person.

Consider the difference between viewing your life from the driver's seat rather than the passenger seat. Imagine the shifts of perspective that happen when you view your life as laying the tracks for the train rather than being in the train. Notice the difference in energy when you say "my life is full" rather than "my life is busy." This simple and mindful shift—to be conscious of the words we use and to look for ways to change our perspective to allow for more power and freedom—is a life-changing practice.

We have beliefs, assumptions, expectations, and general rules for every experience we come up against that create our filter for understanding. The key here is to recognize this human attribute, notice your mental models, and continue to adjust and edit your own to ensure they align with who you truly want to be. Use this power to your advantage! Start with something you know well and love, and see what happens when you use it as a blueprint for something you want to understand, navigate, or inject some more passion and commitment into. Suddenly the unknown or uncertain has some familiarity and a fresh perspective to explore. For example, I love to run long distances and hike mountains. I can use what I know about these endeavors, (i.e., the training, the prep, the mindset, the safety protocol, the research, the adventure, the benefits, the pay-off, the views, the cool down, the recovery and reflection, etc.) to create the action steps needed to take on absolutely any new venture. Start with what you know and trust that you will figure out what else is needed once you are in the work.

(REPEAT AFTER ME)

Fear is a signal from our limbic system telling us (with chemicals rather than words) that something is unknown
or potentially dangerous up ahead.

— • —

When you are actually in physical danger, there often is not time to even think about the danger before you are forced to react. In our day and age, we are flooded with cortisol habitually and unnecessarily.

— • —

Change the way you perceive stress and fear and you build up your body's ability to respond pragmatically and recover efficiently.

— • —

"Eventually you will see that the real cause of problems is not life itself. It's the commotion the mind makes about life that really
causes problems." – Michael Singer

— • —

Today is a new day and you don't have to allow fear to be the backseat driver it strives to be.

— • —

Our negative mind is inherently the first to react. Spend more time and effort in choosing your thoughtful response
after the impulsive reaction.

Reflect, LEARN, GROW

TRY THIS:
Keep a notebook nearby for three consecutive days and record your self-talk patterns. Anytime you feel small, stagnant, fearful, worried, or in self-doubt, write out what you are saying to yourself. Do the same when you are feeling excited, powerful, and full of possibilities. Notice the difference and practice flipping the script on your negative self-talk to find the power, possibility and acceptance in what is.

Build awareness by paying attention to how you talk to yourself. Awareness is the first step to change. You may discover that you are consistently telling yourself things that keep you small or project you into the past or the uncertain future. Practice grounding in the present by creating self-talk that narrates the here and now with openess and acceptance. Learn from the past and get excited about the future, but focus more on what it takes to embrace the space between where you are now and where you want to be.

1. Consider the phrase 'where your mind goes, energy flows.' What does this motivate you to practice?

2. Reflect on your greatest accomplishments in life thus far. What was your relationship with fear in that process? What did you learn from those experiences?

3. When you feel the buzz of cortisol drawing your attention to what could go wrong, what reminders do you need to redirect your mind towards empowerment and pragmatic positivity?

4. What phrases or words are you ready to retire from your vocabulary? What words or phrases will you practice to implement as new habits?

CHAPTER 3: Call to Adventure

"Don't judge each day by the harvest you reap,
but by the seeds you plant."

Robert Louis Stevenson

Every possibility is discovered by one brave leap of faith (2010)

I remember my first "call to adventure." I was six. I was sitting on the stairs next to our steep and narrow driveway in Port Coquitlam, British Columbia, staring out at the summer sky and daydreaming about my life ahead. I became overwhelmed with excitement as I entertained a premonition that I would be a great leader and have a huge impact on the world. As I am sure many people experience at some point in their life, I felt like I was on this earth for a reason larger than me. I wanted my life to make a difference and I felt I had what it takes to lead others in the face of fears and uncertainty. A leader of a tribe of good versus evil. A leader of many as I save lives with my strength and wisdom. I was not scared of this task but rather filled with energy and impatience as I wanted to be that great leader right then. I knew I was too young to take this on immediately yet I was eager and full of hope that my future was going to be bright and beautiful. In that moment, I knew I would do great things in my life.

From that moment on, I unknowingly buried that brave and powerful girl beneath layers of negative self-talk.

Basketball

My dad put up a basketball hoop at the base of our driveway when I was four years old. He and my older brother loved basketball and I, consequently, fell in love with the game. Soon after the hoop was up, I was outside daily to practice and play. One particular day, I was playing one-on-one with my neighbour and best friend, Jordan. His uncle was visiting and came out to watch us. He was a high school basketball coach and after watching us run around and compete like our lives depended on it, he told me that he wanted me to make sure I came to his school when I was old enough. Hearing this positive feedback from a stranger was enough to make me feel like I had a special gift and it was then that I set my first big goal: I was going to be a professional basketball player.

From then on I was obsessed with basketball. All of my excess energy was invested into shooting hoops, playing one-on-one or three-on-three, and practicing my dribbling skills. My identity became intertwined with my pursuit and love of the sport. "My name is Marin and I am a basketball player" is a phrase I used thousands of times to introduce myself.

Every summer I would try out to be on the best team I could find. Each year would get progressively more competitive and I would travel to further destinations to play in tournaments and experience new levels of play. When I was in the fifth grade, my family moved to a rural area west of Calgary, called Springbank. I was lucky to find a group of girls in Springbank that had a passion for basketball similar to my own. These girls were (and still are) gorgeous, hard working, and talented. Despite being best friends and seemingly inseparable, we were also extremely competitive and sometimes cruel to each other, as young girls are known to be. My self-talk habits were rooted in negative comparisons to others. I saw the attention my friends got from boys and I consistently felt like I was not enough.

Now I know that the cortex (outer layer) of our brain does an amazing job at finding the evidence it is looking for. We actually have ten times more neural connections going from our brain to our eyes versus our eyes to our brain (Breuning 2017). What does this mean? We don't just see reality as it is; we see reality filtered through our unique perception, beliefs and assumptions based on what we have experienced and what we are in the habit of seeing. Our brain takes in information from our environment but also fills in a lot from the inside out. Because I came from a pessimistic perspective, with mental models confirming the belief that "I am fat, I am not good enough, and others are prettier and more desirable than me," I gathered a lot of evidence to prove myself right.

Eating Disorder

It was during my high school years that my disordered thoughts around food and body image developed into an eating disorder. I had two older sisters and a mom who all had body and food issues. I remember being seven years old at the swimming pool and consciously sucking in my belly. I saw other girls running around with smiles on their faces and their tummies hanging loose and I was perplexed. They looked so relaxed and didn't seem to be bothered by a round belly. But not me, I kept my tummy tucked in.

Disordered thoughts and behaviour around food is one of the most common struggles in our society. While I have drastically changed my own eating habits and thoughts around food, it is rare to have a day where I do not hear about someone else's disordered relationship with it.

Because I witnessed my sisters and mom struggle with depression and various eating disorders that were extreme in nature, I grew up with a desire to keep my issues "minor." I would binge out of boredom or self-neglect, work out for several hours and then not eat for ten to fifteen hours. This was my daily routine for years. I thought about food and how my body looked more than anything else. I would shame myself while I ate and then shame myself for hours after. I would punish myself with unhealthy food when I was already feeling down, fixate on food when I was bored, and used food to celebrate when I was feeling well. This was a habit that I felt completely trapped by and did not think I would ever overcome.

Mindful Eating

Mindful Eating is a concept and practice that I heard of only a couple of years ago. The mood or mindset we have when we sit down to eat has a direct impact on our ability to digest and absorb nutrients as well as our overall enjoyment and satisfaction in life. Everything is connected. At the root, to be a mindful eater means you slow down and are present with the food you ingest. You are also aware of which foods feel good, and what symptoms or urges can be remedied or amplified by certain foods. As is the case with anything you want to practice: slow down to speed up. If you are feeling anxious or stressed as you prepare to eat or when you ingest your food, your body is in a "fight or flight" state, which is not ideal for this otherwise life-affirming act of fuelling your body. When in this stressed state, our body is preparing for action, so our blood is shunted to our limbs ready to fight or run. Naturally, digestion is bumped down to the bottom of the priority list when in this state.

When I sat at the table looking at my food with worry, guilt and shame, I primed my body to see a threat where there was none. And when I reflected after a meal and felt shame or anger towards myself due to my lack of discipline in eating too much or eating something that was "unhealthy," I amplified this stress response, furthering the degradation of my well-being from the inside out. There is no such things as inherently "good" food or "bad" food. When we demonize our food we are signalling to our own body to prepare for danger. Too much of anything is going to have negative effects over time. We can die from chugging copious amounts of water. But having a treat here and there or letting go of the reins on your healthy diet occasionally is not something to get worked up over.

We can heal this relationship when we honor mealtime with attention and gratitude. The habit I have developed is to slow down the meal process overall. I take time and attention to prepare my food. I sit, not stand, to eat (most of the time). I take a few deep belly breaths as I look at my food, smell it and practice gratitude for the meal, the nourishment, and perhaps the company I am in. I chew my food. I breathe in between bites and put my fork down as a reminder to take in a few deep belly breaths before the next bite. I do my best to only take what I will eat and eat what I take. The simple act of being present with my food and stopping when I feel nourished, has been life-changing for me. I feel proud, connected and encouraged by my mindfulness. While this habit can feel forced and does take conscious effort at first, it becomes the new effortless way of operating once the habit sets in.

Of course, it doesn't always go this smoothly. Sometimes I gulp my meal down and don't clue into my anxious state until my food is gone. I still have the occasional emotional eating episode, where I look to food for comfort, distraction, or to numb whatever else is going on. The main difference in who I am now versus 15-20 years ago is my response to the situation. I realize that it is not the experience that creates a person: it is their relationship to the experience. I take a few moments to reflect on what caused me to slip into this distracted state. I notice how I feel. I make a commitment to myself to slow down, practice self-love, accept that I made a mistake, and then move on. It doesn't ruin my day. It doesn't spiral me into a self-loathing routine. I'm human. I mess up. But one, or two, or three days of poor food choices or behaviour does not set back years of great choices. And if I fall into another slump of years of neglect, I also know I am strong and resilient and will find my way back. So, I let it go.

I remember when I was 16 years old and we had pizza for dinner one night. I was in a numbing mood and ate nine large slices of pizza. I probably would have eaten more but the phone rang and it was for me. A boy I had a crush on was inviting me to go swimming with a group of friends. I declined the offer and made up an excuse of being too busy. I desperately wanted to go and became ashamed and angry with myself for eating so much that I wouldn't dare slip on a swim suit. I remember the negative spiral this took me down and the berating that continued in my mind for days. At the time this felt like the conclusion to all possible intimate relationships, as my mind fixated on the doom-and-gloom scenarios of how my habit to binge would certainly get in the way of deep connections with others. I was so embarrassed and angry, only a bowl of ice cream could join me in my sorrow that night.

In his book, *Nourishing Wisdom*, Marc David refers to the often-overlooked damage we do with our self-talk habits:

"Often, in our attempts to rid ourselves of negative food habits, we adopt strategies that make the conflict about having the habit more damaging than the habit itself."

Having a negative habit is one thing, but we compound the issue by beating ourselves up for having the habit. As I like to say, being disturbed by something is normal, but being disturbed by our disturbances sends you towards an energy-sucking wasteland.

For years I equated "nourishment" only with the food I was ingesting. I saw calories. I saw fat. I saw quantity. I didn't think of my mood, my habits, my self-talk, my relationships or my beliefs as nourishment. But nourishment truly is everything that we surround ourselves with. Marc David draws this out beautifully:

"Biologically, nourishment is encoded in our genes as the body's longing for perpetuation of itself through food and procreation. Psychologically, nourishment is encoded as our longing for perpetuation through creativity, relationship, community, work, and the exchange of ideas. Spiritually, nourishment is encoded as our longing for self-realization. Whether it is a warm meal, a warm fire, a warm friend, or a warm feeling, the metaphoric mind interprets each as nourishment and will substitute food whenever other sources of nourishment run low."

I was running low in all levels of nourishment. I was shallow in my understanding of what it takes to create and sustain happiness and I wasn't giving myself the quality fuel I needed to change my habits.

Growth Mindset vs Fixed Mindset

Looking back, I equate my relatively good behaviour in high school with my commitment to my sport and subsequent lofty goals. I didn't attend many parties, I got drunk less than a handful of times, I didn't get into drugs—other than the occasional social puff of marijuana—and basketball was, overall, still a healthy outlet to burn off teenage angst and boy troubles.

A great mental model to adopt is that of a "growth mindset" or an "investment in loss." This is the ability to focus more on learning, experience, trial and error, and patience in your pursuits. The extreme alternative is a fear-driven mindset that has you invest your time and energy in striving for perfection at all costs, focused solely on being the best, avoiding failure, or the assumption that if it doesn't come easily then it's not a skill you own

Like changing the lens in your glasses and realizing there is a whole new world to perceive and experience, a growth mindset is one that views every moment—good or bad—as an opportunity to explore and generate a wealth of knowledge. It is the realization that you are a work in progress, and perfection is an unrealistic and negative feedback loop that drains precious energy. When you set a goal with a growth mindset, there is no "failure." The goal is always to learn, grow, evolve, discover, and put forth effort while knowing that your own effort is the only thing you can actually control. Growth mindset is focused on one day at a time, one moment at a time, patiently yet actively pursuing your best self and enjoying the process along the way. In the book *Mindset*, Carol Dweck informs us that "[e]ven in the growth mindset, failure can be a painful experience. But it doesn't define you. It's a problem to be faced, dealt with, and learned from."

In a fixed mindset, we get caught up in our initial reactions and do not see the amount of choice and growth available. We get stuck in comparisons, focused solely on being the best, with a desire to be seen or admired. You may believe that the things happening to you or the way you feel can't be changed. This fatalistic approach holds you back from being able to take the steps necessary for change to happen. If you believe you can't change, and you don't invest your effort to learn and grow, your result will be what you predicted. I often am reminded of the Albert Einstein quote: "The definition of insanity is doing the same thing over and over again, but expecting different results." Radical change happens by shifting your mindset and choosing to respond instead of react.

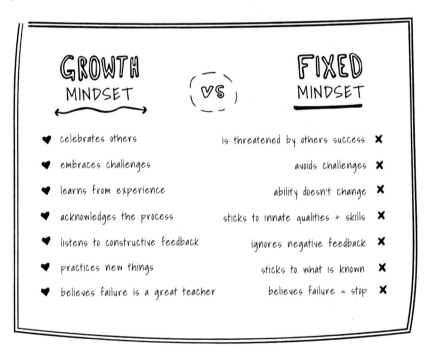

GROWTH MINDSET _vs_ **FIXED** MINDSET

Growth Mindset	Fixed Mindset
♥ celebrates others	is threatened by others success ✘
♥ embraces challenges	avoids challenges ✘
♥ learns from experience	ability doesn't change ✘
♥ acknowledges the process	sticks to innate qualities + skills ✘
♥ listens to constructive feedback	ignores negative feedback ✘
♥ practices new things	sticks to what is known ✘
♥ believes failure is a great teacher	believes failure = stop ✘

Another term I came across recently is an "investment in loss" (Waitzkin 2008). I have found that some people prefer this term to suit their temperament more so than "growth mindset." The slight change of words elicits a different image or mental model of behaviour. It is pertaining to the same mindset, yet the shift in words sparks a shift in perspective. People who "invest in loss" are able to turn stress into excitement and find that sweet spot where stress actually enhances performance. I have many friends who have created a lifestyle that includes putting themselves into situations that push them outside their comfort zone on a daily basis. When I ask if they get nervous, the responses are: "No, just excited." You will believe whatever you repeat. That slight tweak in perspective changes everything. The energy of excitement takes us into a place of possibility. The energy of nervousness points us in the direction of everything that could possibly go wrong. Which energy would you rather have more of? The key is to choose language that feels aligned and inspiring to you.

Tony Robbins says that to create change in our lives we need to understand that 80% of the work is psychological—your mindset—while 20% is strategy[4]. This makes sense to me. I cannot even count how many times I have known what I need to do, had a strategy in place, yet still got stuck in the execution because I somehow talked myself out of the work or exhausted myself with over-thinking before I could take action. When you change your mindset, you change your reality.

For years I thought this concept was impossible for me. I was trapped within the negative and attention-seeking fixed mindset in many areas of my life. You are what you repeatedly do. Your thoughts dictate how you show up, how you feel, and how you relate and connect to yourself and those around you. When I was in the depths of depression, I was demoralized by the notion that my thoughts create my reality because I felt helpless and out of control in my own mind. I had been repeating negative thoughts for years, felt victim to impulsive and intrusive thoughts, and although I knew I needed to focus on the healthy and positive, I felt locked into the patterns I had created.

How do we let go of habits that we didn't realize we chose

---

4   https://www.tonyrobbins.com/podcast/episode-11/

in the first place? How do we build new habits in place of unhealthy yet deeply ingrained old habits? How do we create the energy and motivation for the journey when so much is being used up already? How? We practice. Create structure by focusing on a strong beginning (i.e. a morning routine where you tune into the energy you want more of), and a strong ending (i.e. a nightly routine to reflect on your day and assess what you learned and what momentum looks like for tomorrow).

Allow your mind to tune into the deeper purpose of learning, experiencing and exploring and notice how that outweighs the fear of failure or the pain in the moment. If you are scared to fail you won't get very far in life or you just won't enjoy it as much as you could be.

Although I had a growth mindset when it came to my sport in the beginning, I neglected this kind of strategic and committed mindset when it came to my mental well-being. I was in the gym ready to learn and practice to be the best ball player I could be and was not paying attention to the equally important need to learn and practice stress management, mindfulness, self-love and balance.

What started as a fairly healthy relationship with my sport soon shifted towards the fixed state. I was so committed to my goal of getting a scholarship that I began to place my future happiness in the hands of something external. I can't even count the number of times I thought: "When I get a six-pack, a boyfriend and a full-ride scholarship, then I'll be happy." I believed my depression, anxiety and general self-loathing were products of not working hard enough, not being fit enough, and ultimately, not having what I wanted. My day-to-day mood was directly related to how well I played in my most recent practice or game and how well I had been able to control my urge to binge the night before. It was a vicious cycle.

Recruitment

In the summer between grades nine and ten, my parents sent me to Gilbert, Arizona to live with a family we had met at a tournament. They offered up their home so I could play with their all-star team in a series of big tournaments that Division 1 University scouts attend. It was my first experience with homesickness but it resulted in the beginning of the whirlwind of being recruited. After that summer, I began to receive letters in the mail from schools all across North America. Every week there was a new batch, and I definitely started to feel like my dream was becoming a reality.

The summer after grade ten, my dad and I did a trip down to several schools in the Northwest U.S. to visit campuses and get to know some of the coaches who had been pursuing me, at Weber State in Utah, Boulder Colorado, Pepperdine in Malibu and even Stanford. At the beginning of my grade 11 year, NCAA rules now allowed universities to pay for campus visits so they could roll out the red carpet and dazzle top recruits into signing a contract. I had four trips lined up, and San Diego State University was the first on the list. I had been talking to the head coach for almost a year and felt like he was my uncle and friend. He had stayed at our home for a weekend to watch me play in a tournament and I had spoken to several of the SDSU athletes on the phone as they would come through his office.

My trip to San Diego was my first time seeing the Southern California coast. I fell in love. The campus was the most beautiful I had ever seen. Palm trees. Sunshine. The ocean only ten minutes away. Beautiful people. A new recreation facility with so much space and equipment I could barely take it all in. The team and my coaching staff put on their best performance and I felt like I was immediately a part of a big happy family. My coach expressed how much they needed me and how big a role I would play on this young and vibrant team. I committed and signed a contract before I left for home.

Happiness Baseline

I don't think I stopped smiling for two days straight after that trip. This was a goal I had dreamed about and had been working towards for over a decade. It was only two days after getting home from this magical trip to San Diego that I was struck with an enveloping dark depression. Knowing what I know now, this was the normal down after a big rush of Happy Chemicals, compounded by exhaustion and my typical anxiety. Jonathan Haidt refers to this phenomenon as the "Happiness Baseline" (2006). We often think that when we get something new or something we are working towards, that our happiness will be permanently affected. Or, if we experience heartbreak or tragedy, that our life will be forever less than what it once was. In reality, we all have a set point of happiness (based on DNA, experience, upbringing, and practice) that we bounce back to after the highs and lows of life. We put too much weight into future destinations as if our happiness awaits us but happiness is an inside job. Surprisingly, our happiness levels are not affected long-term by what happens to us. The expectations you have in a situation play a big part in the result of your overall happiness. Because I kept expecting happiness to appear like a badge of honor from achieving a goal, I was continually disappointed and confused when I didn't get what I expected. When your expectations are closely matched to reality, that's when you feel happy. We can't stop our mind's instinct to make predictions and create expectations, both consciously and subconsciously, but we can begin to change the way we perceive life so that our expectations are not getting in the way of our happiness.

For example, some of the ways I have shifted my thinking is to create a mental model of life that reminds me to expect the unexpected, to focus on my effort and my attitude more than on "what happens," and to embrace and love my perfectly imperfect navigation through life.

I did not have these tools of understanding when my expectation of happiness was not sustained after signing my basketball contract. My sadness was made worse by my shock and disbelief that my invisible darkness could reappear even after experiencing one of the biggest highlights of my life thus far. How could I be feeling this way? What was wrong with me? I now see that because I focused, dwelled and attached a story of "something is wrong with me," I turned a normal equilibrium process into a downward spiral.

The quality of your response is directly connected to the

quality of the question asked. The fact that I had been struggling with depression, anxiety and an eating disorder for years was the real issue but because I was also driven, hardworking, passionate, and reasonably social, from the outside it did not appear like I was having an internal struggle. My inner state was in a dire condition and my mindset was feeding fuel into this negative feedback loop.

Rather than being okay with feeling a bit down, I made myself wrong. The feelings amplified and lasted a lot longer than necessary. I am tempted to say that it may have been my "intuition" signalling to me that I had made a huge mistake in signing with SDSU, but I don't believe intuition is anything more than a mixture of fear, desire and experience, and I had no reason to doubt my decision at this point (more on that later). From my perspective, I was heading to San Diego to be a part of a family and achieve my dreams. My coach seemed like a kind and caring man who was excited to have my commitment and would take good care of me. My dad knew a post-Mormon[5] family that lived 20 minutes from the SDSU campus. They expressed the desire to support me in any way they could and offered to lend me their red Miata to get around town in. I was embarking on an adventure and once again, I told myself, I will be happy once I get there.

~

---

5   A label used for people who are no longer affiliated with the Mormon church

Our brain does an amazing job at finding the evidence it is looking for.

———— • ————

The mood or mindset we have when we sit down to eat has a direct impact on our ability to digest and absorb nutrients as well as our overall enjoyment and satisfaction in life.

———— • ————

Honor meal time with attention and gratitude.

———— • ————

It is not the experience that creates a person:
it is their relationship to the experience.

———— • ————

Being disturbed by something is normal, but being disturbed by your disturbances sends you towards an energy-sucking wasteland.

———— • ————

"Whether it is a warm meal, a warm fire, a warm friend, or a warm feeling, the metaphoric mind interprets each as nourishment and will substitute food whenever other sources of nourishment run low."
– Marc David

———— • ————

Radical change happens by shifting your mindset and choosing to respond pragmatically rather than sit in the energy
of the impulsive reaction.

You are what you repeatedly do. Your thoughts dictate how you show up, how you feel, and how you relate and connect to yourself and those around you.

— • —

Happiness is an inside job, and we are not meant to feel elated all the time.

— • —

The quality of your response is directly connected to the quality of the question asked.

Reflect, LEARN, GROW

TRY THIS:

To learn the ways of Mindful Eating, follow the 10-5-1 rule (or 3-2-1 if you need to set the bar lower). Prepare your food with love and care and sit at the table to enjoy. Take ten mindful breaths as you prepare your body to eat and ground yourself in the present moment. This can be done as you finish preparing the food and bring it to the table. Allow your mind to then land on five things you are grateful for today, in this moment. And finish with one big smell of your food. When we slow down and take in our food with our senses, we begin the nourishment process before we even take our first bite.

1. What labels/identity did you perceive yourself and the world through as a child? How did this shape your self-talk patterns or interests?

2. What practices do you have for your spiritual fulfillment? What does spirituality mean to you?

3. Where do you have a growth mindset in your life, and where are you more inclined towards a fixed mindset? How could you practice the growth mindset in all areas of your life?

4. When have you experienced a Call to Adventure in the past? What Call to Adventure are you experiencing today?

CHAPTER 4: Refusal of the Call

"Most of us have two lives. The life we live, and the unlived life within us. Between the two stands Resistance."

The War of Art by Steven Pressfield

My senior year of high school flew by. I had signed my contract for SDSU and I was counting down the days. Although I was extremely excited to get on with my life, I spent a lot of time in contemplation about what could go wrong and how life could be better if I was more attractive, more fun and more disciplined. I judged myself for my exhausting fear-based relationship with food, I struggled with my desire for unattainable perfection, and I spent too much time wondering and worrying about what other people thought of me. I distracted myself with basketball and found solace in the occasional stimulating interaction or conversation but my destructive and draining mind-chatter was the prominent daily experience.

First Painting

For my year-end project in Art 30, I decided to create an oil painting of my nephew Ayden who was born to my eldest sister, who was 20 at the time. Although she had not lived with our family for several years, she moved back when she became pregnant and needed support. I adore Ayden and am continually inspired in many ways by his presence. Creating this painting sparked something inside of me I had never felt before. I had only seen myself as an athlete up to this point, and had few hobbies that brought me into a flow-state, other than basketball. The challenge, patience, attention to detail and pure joy I felt while making that painting made me realize I had other treasures and talents I just hadn't nurtured fully yet.

My grade 12 art project. Oil painting of my nephew Ayden (2004)

Art class was also time to gossip and hang out with a few of my best girlfriends. I remember one particular class I was excited to share news about my latest crush. I had gone to a local university men's basketball game two weekends prior and had been overwhelmed with feelings for one of their star players. There was something about the way this guy moved on the court that I idolized and craved. He was strong, fast, took risks, with a striking smile and intoxicating eyes. He played with such smooth movements and his passion and cockiness was palpable.

Although I judged and compared myself harshly, my competitive nature could trump fear when I was in a good head space. When I was able to set my sights on someone as a challenge, suddenly my self-doubt stepped aside and my desire to "win" took over. I considered this guy to be out of my reach, which made him even more tantalizing.

I was at this particular game with my sister Katie, who had heard me swooning, so she encouraged me to go introduce myself once the game was over. Although intimidated, my pragmatism came

63

into the equation. I truly respected the way he played and I felt that was appropriate enough to take the chance in embarrassing myself. So that's what I did. I went down the stadium stairs as quickly and as stealthily as possible, knowing that most players head off the court immediately after the game to head into the locker room. Fortunately, he was a straggler. I walked up and introduced myself. I told him I admired the way he played and really enjoyed the game. That was it. I turned around and left the stadium feeling brave. I wasn't expecting anything.

You can imagine how shocked and head-over-heels excited I was when he tracked down my email to connect. He expressed his admiration that I was going down to the states to play the following year. He clearly had done his research. We flirted online for a few days and then, finally, he invited me to his apartment to hang out for an evening. I was not emotionally mature enough to step into this relationship with an open heart and an open mind. Instead, I let passion and lust take the wheel. For the next few months, until the end of the summer, I met up with this guy occasionally after basketball practice or as a booty-call after a night out at the bar, and had a blast developing my sexual appetite. This guy was wild and sensuous, and made me feel like a million bucks when I was with him. But I always snuck out once he was asleep, and I didn't allow myself to pursue anything other than a purely sexual relationship. Although this wasn't the healthiest of relationships, it was a lot of fun, and I began to see myself as attractive, sultry and experienced.

Resistance

Despite my initial fear and self-doubt, having someone like him be impressed with me was a nice distraction from my normal routine. Every one of my most profound experiences and positive life-changing choices were first met with a resistance. After there is a "call to adventure," there generally is a moment—or years—of hesitation. It is a programmed impulse that generates fear of the unknown. Fear that things will get worse, will never get better, that you don't deserve what you desire or lack of trust in yourself due to patterns of self-sab-

64

otage. This fear wants you to stay safe by doing nothing and it is our conscious mind that makes up stories and reasons to explain this programmed reaction. This fear drowns you in confusion and loneliness. This fear sees inaction as the lesser of two evils. And right there lies the problem, as this resistance is a path to mediocrity, a path to living life with a constant drain of energy, and a path to losing out on seeing your unique grain of sand have a positive ripple effect in the environment around you.

Whenever my fear or negative self-talk got in the way—which was my normal state for twenty years—I would make choices that kept me small, "protected" or isolated. This "refusal" to show up and stand proud in my body and compassionate in my mind, consistently left me feeling like a shell of a person. I may have struggled with self-doubt and fear, but because I still managed to take chances, I began to notice how good life could feel.

We are programmed to avoid discomfort, but when you know this, you can change your perspective to see this initial resistance to change for what it is: an over-protective system that inherently sees change as a threat to your survival.

Why allow resistance to mold you into the mediocre version of you? Stand tall in your power and trust that even if you fail—or especially when you fail—life opens up to be an even deeper and more pleasurable experience than before. You will learn and grow more than you can imagine when you are aligned in your core values and bold in your actions to create the life of your dreams. Imagine life without sitting in fear, resistance, regret, what-ifs, comparisons and harsh judgements. That is a lot of time and energy freed up for something else.

I have found that before there can be a major transformation in thinking, there needs to be a conversation around forgiveness.

Forgiveness

An interesting dualistic nature I lived with as a child was found in my empathetic, loving, compassionate soul alongside a wicked bully that gained fuel (and entertainment) by laughing at others. I enjoyed making people laugh, and saw easy targets on the backs of anyone I found to be obnoxious in any way. Whether fueled by comedy or emotion, I was a bully.

I was the reason for arms broken, school transfers, and mean nicknames that stuck for years, and you bet there were angry parents calling my house. There was one particular girl in my elementary school that I was quite cruel to. Most of the kids were mean to her, and she became an ongoing target of pranks and random acts of cruelty. Unfortunately for her, I gave off mixed messages. I was kind and showed moments of pure love and connection, but could quickly flip a switch and step over boundaries, highlighting whatever I perceived to be annoying or unpleasant. I inadvertently traumatized her several times because of my mean streak, and made elementary school an occasional nightmare for her.

While it took me until my early twenties to track this girl down and apologize, there were many other people in my life that I verbally abused. What makes me feel awful is the adult understanding that children are developing programming that they most likely will use and be affected by for the rest of their life. It pains me to think that someone out in the world is living in a prison of negative thinking as a result of some of the things I said or did as a child.

It wasn't just schoolyard kids that felt my wrath. My younger siblings were often easy targets for torment to relieve my boredom or distract from my own pain. I have had several conversations with two of my younger siblings specifically, who I was such a beast to.

It is what it is. While I regret being the reason for others' pain, I do not shame, blame or condemn myself for being a bully. I feel empathy for the people I harmed, I feel sadness for being the cause of negative self-talk habits in my younger siblings, and I know that what matters most is what I do with this awakening. I feel the light of love and passion within me. I see the curious and animalistic young girl who learned poor habits early on and masked her self-doubt by poking fun at others. I feel her pain too.

When I reflect on my mindset and psychology as that young lost girl, I see the duality and confusion that plagued my own naive mind. How I treated other people was a reflection of how I treated myself. Even after apologizing to a few select people who were at the brunt of my cruelty for years, I still had a cycle of shame as I judged myself for being a "bad" person.

What I discovered was that my slips in integrity were causing immense amounts of pain in my mind and body. While it was fun in the moment to be cruel, I did not feel good about myself after the fact, and would often become plagued with guilt and sadness for the remainder of the day. When I was young, I didn't know any better. I developed a habit to entertain and elevate myself at the expense of others' comfort, but as I got older, and "knew better," this way of being no longer fueled me whatsoever.

The problem is, a deeply ingrained habit that has been in operation for years has a way of keeping a grip on your psyche. While I was able to reflect on my past and apologize to those I hurt, I still had a tendency to take advantage of people or situations when I felt I could gain something or was owed something. Especially when I was tired or stressed out, I would have an urge to be greedy or selfish, to attempt to be a puppet-master of sorts and manipulate those around me, and to blame others when I found myself in a triggered state. My biggest struggles, and consequent growth spurts, were the result of this ego-driven storytelling that I need more than what I have or that success is found in manipulation. This pattern pushed me into greediness or gossip that served to make me feel better about myself.

Every time I allowed myself to go into those low vibration states I would feel awful soon after. It was like I had finally realized I was allergic to a certain food but kept eating it day after day, albeit in smaller doses each time.

Slowly, layer after layer, as I faced my own hypocrisy and re-committed to my core values and purpose, I developed the awareness to pause when I was faced with an opportunity to let my triggers or compulsions overpower me. I could pause long enough to ask myself

"How do I want to feel at the end of the day when I lay my head down?" And, "What course of action here will support me to get there?" Each time I made the choice to act out of integrity, I had to face my own hypocrisy, reflect and feel the pain I had stepped into, spend time and energy to redirect my course, apologize or ask for a do-over, and forgive myself with the reminder that I am not supposed to be perfect. While this series of steps is important, it takes a lot of energy. I want efficiency. I would much rather save my precious time and energy for other things and live aligned and powerful in my core values and higher purpose.

Self-Discipline

I needed discipline and reminders to keep me on a path of compassion and forgiveness towards myself. Rather than training for a race or a big game, I trained and developed discipline in how I talked to and treated myself.

In yoga philosophy, we learn that self-discipline is translated in the ancient language Sanskrit as "tapas," which means "heat." It is as though self-discipline suggests a burning of the old to make way for the new. Through heat we transform.

In the book *The Yamas and Niyamas* by Deborah Adele, she asks us, "can we grow our ability to stay in the fire and let ourselves be burned until we are blessed by the very thing that is causing us the pain and suffering?" Through the practice of self-discipline, we are faced with what is uncomfortable and keeps us stagnant. We have the choice to allow what breaks us down to also break us open and, ultimately, create a breakthrough. When we embrace the uncertainty all around us, and remind ourselves that change takes time, attention and trial and error, we can bring some softness and patience into the equation. The goal is not to be fearless or avoid pain at all costs, but rather, to be able to breathe through and embrace the darkness in order to give the light more depth, beauty and polarity.

Life throws curve-balls. Death and tragedy will strike all around you. Prepare yourself to grow and gain resilience by training yourself to stay with what is unpleasant. See it as a gift, and lean in to learn and explore what your reactions and compulsions are trying to teach you. This is where your transformation awaits.

When we can step back and notice our thoughts, we begin to notice patterns. We learn to detach from the emotional pendulum swing and let go of the stories we make up with assumptions and judgments that are simply unnecessary. When we change our mindset to observe without judgment, we begin to see where our "dis-ease" truly comes from: our own thoughts and actions.

Deborah Adele continues,

"Our minds are like the river carrying things in it. If we identify with what the mind is carrying - thoughts, stories, beliefs - then we will think we are those things. However, if we identify with the Divine within us (the pure river) and merely watch the thoughts float by, we will know we are simply carrying the thoughts, stories and beliefs; they are not who we are" (2009).

Balance

I know this has entered your mind before: "I need more balance in my life." What does that really mean? How do we achieve balance? What does it feel like? How do we get our own mind, our boss, our family, our friends, and our partners to value and honour our balance?

Balance is a dance. It is the middle point between extremes and it shifts and evolves as much as we do ourselves. Our universe is ever-expanding and we are products of our universe. It is the contrast between light and dark, up and down, happy and unhappy, life and death, that makes life the beautiful and unpredictable journey that it is. Balance within this expansion is constantly shifting and so too must our understanding and playfulness with balance. Finding balance day to day is a practice. It is achieved when you are able to let go of blame, embrace imperfection, and get comfortable with uncertainty. It is the dance between desire for more and contentment and gratitude for what is. It is a give and take but without force or need. It is walking a tight rope and knowing that if you over-think, over-analyze, tense up, or allow yourself to get distracted, you will lose your balance. But just as easily, with one mindful and pure breath, you can also find your balance. And perhaps this continual loss and discovery or recreation of a sense of balance is integral to truly understanding this jewel of life.

In yoga philosophy, balance is often understood as effort and surrender, which are described as "two wings of the same bird" (Adele 2009). The dynamic between the two can be segmented in time slots throughout your day, or can be as quick and fluid as your *inhale* (the effort) and your *exhale* (the surrender).

In our desire to do more, be more, accomplish more, and be seen as more, we can easily lose sight of the importance of acknowledging ourselves, loving who we are, and embracing each precious moment for what it is.

When you can step back from the emotional pendulum swing, observe without judgment, and stick to the brass tacks of what the moment presents, suddenly you have more energy to live, love, and problem solve.

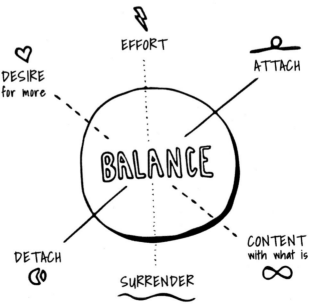

Many of us do not have the option to take several days off whenever we feel like it and I think it is important to note that balance does not require a full day of playing hooky. Balance is found in mindful moments. Balance is presence. It is acknowledging how you feel right now so you can take steps to ensure you stay between the extreme pendulum swings of emotions or actions.

Engage with action and effort, and make time to step back and embrace some release and surrender. The more extreme we are in our thoughts and actions, the less forward momentum we will actually create. The skeleton key here—again—is to slow down to speed up.

One of the best quotes I have discovered in my search for balance is from the book *The Laws of Spirit* by Dan Millman,

"If gravity is the glue that holds the universe together, balance is the key that unlocks its secrets. Balance applies to our body, mind, and emotions, to all levels of our being. It reminds us that anything we do, we can overdo or underdo, and that if the pendulum swings too far to one side, it will inevitably swing to the other."

I finished high school in June 2004 and was awarded Miss Basketball Alberta, an exciting privilege considering the past recipients were some of my idols who had also gone on to play basketball at big universities. I felt I was finally stepping into myself and was excited for the opportunities ahead. I was now taking a prescription of Dexadrine to help with my anxiety, but had not dealt with my ongoing depression or eating disorder. I had convinced myself that my problems would all melt away once I was in a new city and living my "dream life." I was ready for the new me, for the opportunity to play the sport I love and to get the accolades I thought I deserved. Looking back, I can see that I was a ticking time bomb. I had developed the habit of avoiding my demons, numbing my pain with food and exercise, and placing my future happiness in the hands of an outside source "down the road." A recipe for disaster.

My trophies for Miss Basketball Alberta (2004)

(REPEAT AFTER ME)

We are programmed to avoid discomfort, but when you know this, you can change your perspective to see this initial resistance to change for what it is: an over-protective system that inherently sees change as a threat to your survival.

——— • ———

When you allow yourself to feel whatever is coming up for you, it will pass through you and open you back up to the moment, where your higher Self is patiently waiting.

——— • ———

What you resist, persists.

——— • ———

"Being content with our discontentment is itself a gateway to the calm depths within."
— Deborah Adele

——— • ———

How you treat others is a reflection of how you treat yourself.

——— • ———

"Can we grow our ability to stay in the fire and let ourselves be burned until we are blessed by the very thing that is causing us the pain and suffering?" — Deborah Adele

——— • ———

When we change our mindset to observe without judgment, we begin to see where our "dis-ease" truly comes from: our own thoughts and actions.

When you can step back from the emotional pendulum swing, observe without judgement, and stick to the brass tacks of what the moment presents, suddenly you have more energy to
live, love and problem solve.

Slow down to speed up.

Balance is the dance between desire for more and contentment and gratitude for what is.

Reflect, LEARN, GROW

TRY THIS:

     Choose one thought-cycle that you are not happy with; for example: judgement, self-doubt, pessimism, shame, etc., or a word that you want to remove from your vocabulary. In The 4-hour Work Week, Timothy Ferriss suggests using a bracelet to stand as your reminder for these tough thought patterns. Anytime you notice yourself in that thought cycle or when you use that word, move the bracelet to the opposite wrist. To get it back on the wrist it started on (which is the goal for the end of the day) you must consciously shift your mind and change your wording to approach the situation with love, acceptance, and kindness. You may be moving that bracelet several times in the day, but after a couple of days you will notice your awareness is heightened and you will have more conscious energy guiding your mind to change the habit to serve the new direction of your choosing.

1. Give yourself permission to be imperfect and choose to forgive your own missteps, wrongdoings or regrets. What have you been holding onto when you have the ability to let go, forgive and grow?

2. With whom are you competing—or behaving as though you are? How can you change that relationship to be one that empowers both of you and brings in the energy of abundance and collaboration?

3. Reflect on someone or a situation that triggers you into a low-vibration or disturbed state. What is that trigger bringing up from inside of you that needs attention and healing? What we see in others is a reflection of what is going on inside of ourselves. What can you learn about yourself by noticing what disturbs you in others?

4. Where in your life do you need to focus on TRUST and let go of control?

CHAPTER 5: Crossing the Threshold into a New World

"Creative work is not a selfish act or a bid for attention on the part of the actor. It's a gift to the world and every being in it. Don't cheat us of your contribution. Give us what you've got."

The War of Art by Steven Pressfield

Air Geordie (2014)

First Day on Campus

My first day on the San Diego State University campus was surreal. I had waited for this day for years and it was finally here. I kept on a brave and confident demeanor as I moved through the motions of acquainting myself with campus, but beneath the surface my anxiety was building. My three roommates were the other three rookies on my team, one from Orange County, one from Utah, and the other from Texas. All four of us were living away from home for the first time in our relatively privileged lives. Our first few interactions were extremely positive as we rallied together as rookies, roommates and birds leaving the nest. In the afternoon, we met with our coaching staff to go over our schedule for the next couple of months.

The NCAA has many rules—which change yearly—as an attempt to keep things fair, and not allow coaches to overwork their athletes. During our preseason, as long as our coaches were present, the first few practices we had as a team could not involve a ball. This meant a lot of running, defence drills, and scrimmaging plays without the satisfaction of dribbling or seeing the ball go in the hoop. A ball could be added in when there were only four players present with our coaching staff, as long as we stuck to half court. Once the coaches left the gym, we could play full court with the ball. After a few weeks of that, we then could move to regular three-hour practices and training sessions. Once into October, we could begin exhibition games against other teams. The season didn't officially start until the end of December, which meant four months of practice and strength training before any regular season games. I began to hate the concept and idea of practice.

Student Athlete

This was much harder than I imagined it would be. Although I had been training for this for years, the reality was I was not healthy in my mind, which was creating issues in my body—compounded by my eating disorder, which left me less than equipped for this experience. My sport had become my job, I was not loving the job or myself, and my passion for the game was slowly being sucked dry. I was no longer excited to lace up my shoes. It became a chore, a nuisance, another task to get through in the day.

As Student Athletes, our entire day was planned out from 6am until 8pm at night. Each morning we had a cardio workout on the field, followed by strength training in the weight room, and then straight to class for 8am. The rest of the morning and afternoon was spent going from one class to the next, and at 3pm we are back in the gym to warm up and practice until 630pm. Ice baths and often team meetings were held after practice. Once I showered, had dinner, and attempted to do some homework, it was time to head to bed and do it all over again.

After a couple weeks of this, I would waddle into my 8am class with ice saran-wrapped to my legs. I don't remember the topic of that class. The first half of the hour I was focused on enjoying stillness while breathing through the aches and pains in my body. The second half of class was spent peeling off the saran wrap and ice as quietly as possible, which was nearly impossible.

I was extremely homesick and made matters worse by being introverted and solely focused on basketball. I did not think about balance, fun, friends or quality me-time. All I cared about was being the best and all I saw was how far I was from being the best. Any free time I had I would spend in the gym or isolated in my room.

A few issues arose as the rookie apartment was learning how to live with each other. One of my roommates would leave the microwave door wide open after each use. This agitated me to the point of walking in and slamming that door shut with anger and disdain. I wasn't sleeping well, I was anxious all day counting down the minutes until practice, and I was focused on the fact that I was unhappy and exhausted day after day.

I thought that once the season actually started and we would travel every other weekend for away games, then I would be happy. To practice and train without playing consistent games for four months was almost more than I could bear.

But of course, placing my happiness on future expectations and not paying attention to my role in my own happiness in this moment would once again prove to make my life harder. The pre-season games started and I didn't get much play time. I would over-analyze my every move on the court and read into every look or lack of acknowledgment from my coaching staff. Once I was subbed off I would immediately feel sorry for myself.

I was up to the heaviest weight I had ever been, a 6'0" girl at 165lbs, and I was more muscular than I had ever been. Despite my strength, I fatigued quickly due to my poor nutrition and mental health state. In November, my coach pulled me aside and told me he thought I would benefit if I could lose some weight. To be honest, I don't remember the exact words he used in this conversation but all I heard was "you're fat." He asked me to get on the treadmill a couple times a week for some extra cardio. I was shocked by this request. I was exhausted with the schedule I was expected to keep already, and I couldn't imagine where I was supposed to fit in an extra cardio workout. I took this sad report back to some of my veteran teammates. They empathized and rolled their eyes at my coaches lack of female understanding as they shared similar stories from their recent coach interactions. Our coach was not who I thought he was. Or, as I see it now, he didn't handle the stress of being a Division 1 women's coach very graciously. I began to hear stories from my teammates of how he treated them and why some of their teammates transferred out the year before. I started to realize that he was not the mentor and "dad figure" that he so proudly claimed to be while recruiting me. Even his smile was aggressive. He was angry and stressed out more often than not. I saw the effects this had on his coaching staff. As the season progressed, there were more outbursts of negative emotion from everyone.

Negative Self-Talk

I remember one particular game, I was subbed in and I was playing really well, from my perspective at least. I scored a few baskets, got a few rebounds, was playing solid defense, and I finally felt some strength and resilience in my movements. I was subbed off and high-fived all the way down the bench. I sat with the expectation of getting put back on in a few minutes. But, as William Shakespeare said, "expectation is the root of all heartache." I sat. And sat. And sat. Demoralized and angry, I was put back on in the final few minutes of the game when we were down by 25 points. The buzzer went and I was livid and emotionally defeated. Once on the bus back to our hotel, I got up the nerve to talk to one of my assistant coaches who was in charge of substitutions that game. I expressed my perception of playing really well and then not seeing any play time until the final few minutes. He admitted that he had forgotten about me. Whether this was true or not, I allowed myself to get eaten up by that response; "I'm worthless," "I'm forgettable," "I don't matter," "What's the point?"

What matters most is our thoughts. Our thoughts create the neurochemical soup that our mind and body steep in. My soup was toxic. I had created a habit in my thinking that was rapidly emptying my energy tank on a daily basis. I focused on what I didn't want. I thought about all the ways I was unhappy. I dragged my feet across campus consumed by anxiety about what had happened in the past and what I was nervous about in the future. I created a prison in my thinking. My life was something to put up with and I wanted to escape.

Conscious and Subconscious

It is important to understand how and why we fall into patterns of negative self talk and habits that impede our growth and diminish our joy. Only from a place of awareness in seeing the structure of the system as well as our unique habits within the system can we create the change we desire. Deep down, our objectives are quite simple; avoid pain and seek pleasure. Our subconscious system is always in pursuit of these basic needs, and fires up a danger signal whenever a "threat" is perceived through any of the senses, which could be triggered from something as simple and common as shallow breathing. A threat is anything that remotely hints at you losing something you want or need; and we "need" safety, a sense of belonging, and a feeling that we matter. Often you will not be consciously aware of the actual cause of the stress response that is triggered, but our conscious mind will make up a story to explain it because we have learned "knowing is safer that not knowing." This brilliantly over-protective system then ends up being a force of harm rather than good, as we can fall victim to limiting beliefs and create a stress-riddled inner-environment.

What we now know about the human brain as a result of recent discoveries in neuroscience is still only a fraction of the full depth and gravity of truly understanding how our brains work. While disagreements still run through this field of science and new insights are shared and suggested, I choose to pay attention to science that guides me towards integration of all parts, open systems that leave room for uncertainty, and an inspiring quality that sparks empowerment and hope, and of course, I aim to be aligned with the general consensus of the scientific population.

The subconscious mind is housed in the evolutionarily older area called the limbic system (or reptilian brain). The outer layer—called the *cortex*—is the more recently evolved conscious mind, which is what we refer to as our higher-self, as this is where we solicit reason and direction. It is the conscious mind that seeks development and to be driven by a higher purpose. The conscious mind has gifted us the ability to be pragmatic in the face of an emotional reaction and to see choice above and beyond impulses and habits. It is the catalyst of our evolution into beings who can think past automatic, animalistic reactions, to make choices aligned with who we truly want to be versus who we were raised, programmed or accidentally habituated to be.

Our subconscious is impulsive, animalistic and habitual. It communicates with neurochemicals triggered by environmental factors and the compounding result of self-talk. The subconscious system doesn't discern between healthy or destructive habitual thought patterns, reactions or behaviors. In other words, it does not concern itself with quality of life; rather, it reacts instinctively to what it has learned, repeated, and what conserves energy (i.e., what is a habit) as these are the patterns that have allowed you to survive thus far.

We are subconsciously driven approximately 95% of the day, while our conscious mind takes the helm the remaining 5% of the time. This saves us a lot of energy, in theory, but if you are not conscious of the power and influence of your subconscious, it is like you are trying to operate a giant ship while only having access and awareness of 5% of the vessel.

In the book *The Happiness Hypothesis,* Haidt introduces us to these two major players in our brain as The Elephant (subconscious) and The Rider (conscious). Haidt tells us,

"The automatic system (aka Elephant) has its finger on the dopamine release button. The controlled system (aka Rider), in contrast, is better seen as an advisor. It's the rider placed on the elephant's back to help the elephant make better choices" (2006).

This analogy has become one of the most influential ideas I have encountered, and continue to use to this day. It speaks volumes to imagine your consciousness as a human rider atop a six-ton elephant. In a battle of wills and strength, who do you think comes out the victor? To generate a relationship between these two important parts of your brain, it requires a deep understanding of how the two systems work, along with some finesse, patience and a calm soothing voice.

When I feel the inner battle—a deep desire for instant gratification and avoidance of change, simultaneously with a desire to grow and invest more in delayed gratification—I can feel the tug-of-war between these two systems.

While these two parts of the brain are deeply interconnected, they are not on speaking terms, per se. Your Rider (consciousness) is where your self-talk resides. While you have choice in your self-talk, we are programmed to be creatures of habit. So, regardless of the quality of your self-talk, today you will repeat approximately 95% of what you thought yesterday. The way you talk to yourself dictates how you feel because your choice of words points in a positive or negative direction which your subconscious then matches with good or bad feeling chemicals. While your self-talk patterns influence the chemicals released in your body, inversely, chemicals are released constantly and your conscious mind makes up stories to explain the feelings your neurochemicals create. We are meaning making machines. For example, when you consciously remind yourself what you are proud of and what you are grateful for, you may notice your shoulders roll back, you stand a little taller, and a feeling of awe, respect and contentment washes over you. On the other hand, let's say you are sitting in a coffee shop and you notice an old acquaintance sitting a few tables away from you. You catch their gaze and send a smile their way, but this person doesn't return the smile and turns away. Even though you have limited evidence to suggest that lack of acknowledgment has anything to do with you, your subconscious will register that as an unmet offer for connection and cortisol will be signalled to grab your attention and make you feel low or anxious. This is the pivotal moment. Your self-talk will match that vibration and begin by saying something like "I am unnoticeable," "I am insignificant," or "that person is terrible." Without the knowledge that this is a natural reaction, you might get stuck in that low vibration feeling and allow the rest of your day to be viewed through the lens of that perception. However, with an understanding of our biology, you can feel that reaction and then remind yourself you don't have enough evidence to make that assumption and in general, people are consumed by their own "stuff," it is most likely that person didn't register the gaze, the smile or the familiar face. You can't control your subconscious reactions, but you can control your response after that reaction. Your Elephant (subconscious) communicates solely with neurochemicals flowing down neural pathways. When those pathways are paved well and used often, that energy flows with ease (i.e., the path of least resistance). When the pathway has not been used before or is not used often, it takes more energy to move down that pathway, which creates a feeling of discomfort and resistance. This tells you nothing about the *quality* of whatever you are engaging in; remember, all your subconscious knows is what is comfortable and has kept you alive so far.

The drama and storytelling that can ensue are more than enough to keep you occupied in your own little world, exhausted by the mind-chatter and impulsive swings, and stagnant in life due to the mediocrity our subconscious craves for comfort and safety. Your brain continues to flow energy down these same neural pathways, which leads you towards the same types of relationships and cycles through the same types of thoughts, until you carve new ones, through conscious and deliberate repetition or by accident through life-trauma or mindless living. Basically, you can live by accident, subject to your subconscious patterns and impulses, or you can see the wisdom, strength and power of your conscious mind and pave new pathways to deliberately create the habits you desire.

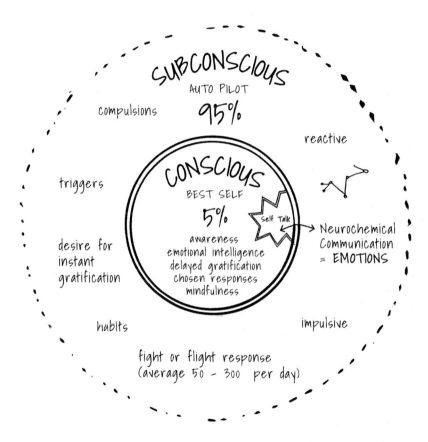

Ideally, we want these two systems to work together. The motivation and energy we get from the subconscious, along with the direction, purpose and connections we can foster with our conscious, is a powerful combination. When we are directed solely by our Elephant, we are piloted by unreasonable emotion. When our Rider takes the lead, we can spin our wheels, over-thinking every situation, exhausting ourselves with options until we have drained our energy and capacity to move forward. While our Elephant has way more power than the Rider (40 nerve impulses per second in the cortex versus 40 million nerve impulses per second in the limbic system), we can learn to notice our habitual reactions and choose to respond with direction, purpose and self-discipline (when we have the energy to do so) (Lipton 2013).

This is where mindfulness and effort comes into the picture. "Consciousness is merely a bystander observing a decision already taken, almost like watching ourselves on video—with the power to 'veto' when mindful of doing so" (Coates 2012).

The busier and noisier your mind is, the less able you are to be present and mindful in the moment at hand. When we are in a state of stress or stuck in the internal ramblings of our own mind, our higher levels of consciousness are shut off and we revert to our deeply programmed paths of least resistance, leading us to react on autopilot. Just like my dad and his must-wear-socks-in-the-house-rule.

As John Ratey says in *Shadow Syndromes*, "What stress is to the body, noise is to the brain." This is why I practice meditation daily. Something as simple as one minute focused on deep belly breaths while I gift myself space to be content and present with what is, is enough to build a stronger neural pathway towards calm. Meditation is the simplest and most accessible path to my higher self. From this place of stillness, softness, peace and contentment, my consciousness is fueled and my subconscious calms down.

Understanding these two separate but harmonious parts of our brain will allow you to take a step back and observe your thoughts, reactions, emotions, and triggers with a new sense of appreciation and clarity. We need to practice mindfulness and acceptance in order to conserve the energy needed for these two parts of the brain to work together. You cannot force the Elephant to do what the Rider wants to do. In fact, attempting to create change through force or willpower alone can have the opposite effect, making the instinct or habit you want to leave behind even stronger. If you are a smoker, and you decide to stop cold-turkey and force yourself to change, not only will the process be painful and lack joy, you have a much higher chance of relapse. You can face a change with fear as your driver, but that almost guarantees that fear will be with you at the finish line. You can choose to face change with love and appreciation for where and who you are, and bring more healing energy and joy into the journey. It's all a matter of what you consciously choose to bring along with you. If you are approaching change from a place of not being good enough, then you may reach your desired goal to realize that the sense of lack and "not-enough-ness" is still knocking. Your mindset matters.

So how do we get our automatic and animalistic Elephant and our pragmatic and forward-thinking Rider to work together?

In the book *Switch*, by brothers Dan and Chip Heath, we are introduced to a three-step process to align the Elephant and Rider, get out of our own way and enable the unique brilliance of collaboration and harmony to take effect. We need to direct the Rider, motivate the Elephant, and shape the path.

Direct the Rider

Without a clear vision and direction, you will jump from one "good idea" to the next, victim to what feels good in the moment rather than what will get you to your desired destination. When you set goals you are proud of and inspired by with a higher purpose you are working towards, your Rider can be much more convincing and your Elephant becomes easier to tame. Feed your Rider fuel by continuing to learn, edit your current mental models and adapt new ones that use language and metaphors that light you up inside and out. Engage in conversations about ideas and experiences rather than gossip or surface level small-talk. Focus on scripting out the critical moves that will continue momentum forward, have a clear destination in mind (even if that destination is a feeling), and realign with your purpose weekly by setting an intention and breaking your work down into actions that will allow small wins and rewards. Your conscious mind wants to know where you are headed so it can more skillfully guide your Elephant.

Motivate the Elephant

Our Elephant is emotional, impulsive, reacts on deeply ingrained programming and is one million times stronger than its counterpart the Rider. This is why we are all so familiar with the feeling of knowing what we want to do but just not being able to make ourselves do it. To work with your Elephant, you have to coax it and gently guide it. The imagery of this metaphor is purposeful in its use of a human Rider on top of a six-ton Elephant. When the Elephant feels stuck or when it becomes out of control, good luck trying to stop, drag, or push this animal. There needs to be a relationship and there needs to be a healthy amount of internal motivation. Every creature responds well to love, appreciation and compassion, including our own animalistic nature. It is vital for you to understand what your Elephant needs to keep calm and content, for example: sleep, nourishment, sweat, safety, connection, purpose, mindful movement, meditation, rewards and time to play.

When you have a deep-rooted sense of WHY and a clear vision of what you are working towards, your Elephant is fuelled by Happy Chemicals (i.e., dopamine, serotonin, and oxytocin) that keep you engaged and feeling good. When you have purpose behind your actions you are more likely to keep your Elephant invested in the task at hand. And when you take care of yourself by getting enough sleep, eating a balanced and healthy diet, working up a sweat several times a week, honoring and growing the relationships you keep and acknowledging the progress and gratitude in your life daily, you are providing the fuel your Elephant needs to be a high-functioning system for mindful living.

The Elephant is basically your child-like self that is stuck in adolescence. It likes to feel good and works best when you allow yourself time to breathe in your accomplishments and surround yourself with inspiration and positivity. Find the feeling you are working towards, and allow that to motivate your actions.

Shape the Path

Once these two are aligned and working together, you will have more energy and a deeper connection to who you are. Set yourself up for success by tweaking your environment to be conducive to the change you seek in your life. Surround yourself with inspiring and empowering people who will challenge and support you. Leave reminders for yourself. Organize your living and working space to offer the energy and reminders you need. Take time daily to reconnect with your vision, celebrate your progress, redirect your aim when you notice you've lost your way, and tap into what energy you need to bring balance into your day.

This journey is about the long game. Where do you want to be five, ten, or twenty years from now? How do you want to feel? What habits do you want to leave in your past and what habits do you want to adopt in their place? Tackle one habit at a time by focusing on the positive things you want to bring into your life, instead of focusing your energy on the habits you are trying to let go of. As you see positive habits show up in your life, your negative habits tend to lose power and melt away. Bring mindfulness and contentment into the journey and continue the practice of letting go of the thought that your happiness awaits at some future destination.

The Elephant + The Rider

Change takes time, and repetition is the only sure-fire way of creating intentional and purposeful change. Building new circuits leading to new habits takes at least three weeks of daily repetition. Your brain resists new habits as an attempt to conserve energy, regardless of their potential for good. You can know something is healthy and eagerly want to adopt it in your repertoire, but your energy comes from your Elephant, which speaks in chemicals; although novelty feels good at first, once it is clear that you are attempting to detour energy down a new pathway when a superhighway is available, this is registered as a threat. Ingrained neural connections save energy in the short term, and your Elephant is concerned only with instant gratification. With this perspective, when you feel resistance to change creep into your mind, you can view that as a sign that you are in an important phase of the change process. Send some compassion and appreciation to the part of you that is trying to keep you safe, and then recommit and continue down the path to the change you seek.

"In time we become what we most believed about ourselves. And in doing so, we created a wall, which for most of us will stand invisibly but powerfully between us and our unlimited futures for as long as our old programming remains in force. Unless the programming we received is erased or replaced with different programming, it will stay with us permanently and affect and direct everything we do for the rest of our lives."

What to Say When you Talk to Yourself by Shad Helmstetter

A painting I made to represent the tricky Elephant mind and how change works. It is not an upward trajectory; it ebbs and flows, dips and dives, loops and swirls. In the moment it can feel like you are moving backward, but when you take a step back and assess progress you can see your direction is moving upward and onward (2013)

~

(REPEAT AFTER ME)

Our thoughts create the neurochemical soup that our mind and body steep in.

— • —

You can't control your subconscious reactions, but you can control your response after that reaction.

— • —

Without a clear vision and direction, you will jump from one "good idea" to the next, victim to what feels good in the moment rather than what will get you to your desired destination.

— • —

Every creature responds well to love, appreciation and compassion, including our own animalistic nature.

— • —

Once the Elephant and Rider are aligned and working together, you will have more energy and a deeper connection to who you are.

— • —

When you feel resistance to change creep into your mind, you can view that as a sign that you are in an important phase of the change process. Keep going!

Reflect, LEARN, GROW

1. What experience have you had in Crossing the Threshold into a New World?

2. Where in your life have you given away your power to someone who abused the responsibility they had as a potential mentor? What beliefs or self-talk patterns did you buy into as a result?

3. Consider the steps to align your Conscious Mind (Rider) and your Subconscious Mind (Elephant):

   a) What are your goals for 1 year from today—direction, focus, health, career, growth, learning, etc. ?

b) WHY? What is your motivation for working towards these goals? What growth-minded reminders do you need to keep yourself focused on what truly matters (versus what comparisons, fears, and self-sabotage bring to mind)?

c) What key steps come first? What are the small, incremental steps this week? What will you do to tweak your environment to support the inspiration, pathway, and joy for the journey?

CHAPTER 6: Magical Mentor

"It is all forward progress, even when it seems like
everything is falling apart."

The Gift of our Compulsions by Mary O'Malley

Faces (2008)
We are the combination of the five people we spend the most time with. Take a step
back and consider who you surround yourself with

Christmas time in San Diego was approaching and my family
decided to rent a condo on the beach for one week over the holiday.
I was allotted only two days off—Christmas Eve and Christmas Day—
and would fly to Texas on Boxing day for an exhibition game. I attached
myself to my siblings and parents like a wounded puppy. I felt like I
could breathe for the first time since arriving in San Diego. My parents
had heard my cries of disappointment and sadness over the phone for
months, and my tune had not changed. They did their best to console
me and assure me I would be fine. Those two days flew by and I sulked
and felt sorry for myself for most of it. When I headed back to the
gym for Boxing Day practice I was even more unhappy than before. I

travelled to Texas with my team but wanted nothing more than to stay in that condo on the beach with my family.

I Quit

It was the game in Texas that tipped me over the edge. Looking back now, I can see that I was carrying every criticism, every negative belief, every self-doubt, every regret, and every unmet expectation on my back and was clueless in how to let them go. I felt like I was boiling over with a dark cloud above my head.

Early in the game, I was a part of a play that didn't go well and my coach called a timeout. I was pulled aside by one of our assistant coaches who angrily explained what I did wrong. Once he concluded his rant, I began walking back to the bench and he must have not been particularly pleased with my demeanor so he pushed me from behind to move a little quicker. I do not believe he meant to push me as hard as he did and, had I been in a better mindset, I probably would have shrugged it off, but that was not the case. I sat down on the bench and looked around to see if anyone saw what just happened. I was alone in that experience and felt smaller and more worthless than ever. I realize now that a big part of my problem was my inability to address things head on and, even more than that, my inability to let things go. This occurrence truly was the straw that broke the camel's back. In that moment, I gave up.

We flew back to San Diego and my family had a few days left on their Christmas vacation. I moved into their condo and told my parents that I was done. I was not able to put myself through this anymore. I told them my many reasons to quit, including the final "push" at the game in Texas. My dad contacted my coach to explain the situation and scheduled a meeting that I was told I must attend. I was terrified but with my dad by my side I mustered the courage to face the man that I was disappointing and abandoning mid-year. We arrived at my coach's office and my assistant coach, the one whom I had accused of pushing me, was also there. Neither one of them looked happy.

We sat opposite of each other, separated only by a small

wooden coffee table. I braced myself for an uncomfortable conversation. It started with my assistant coach confronting me about my accusation. "I never laid my hands on you," he said. I tried to explain that I understand he probably did not mean to push me as hard as he did but he did put his hand on my back and push me toward the bench as I walked away from him. He denied this over and over and he did not even hint at an apology. I was not accusing him of abusing me and I was giving him the benefit of the doubt but still he did not budge. I simply became quiet and allowed him to have the last word.

I explained to my coaches that I was unhappy and exhausted and, although I was not sure if I would come back, I expressed my need to go home. Despite their assurances that it's not as bad here as I am making it sound and that I would regret leaving, I was solid in my decision and there was no way I could be convinced to stay. We said our goodbyes and I told them I would let them know my final decision in a few days.

I walked out of that meeting shaking. I was thrilled to feel the sense of freedom but in shock at the same time. The last couple of days in San Diego with my family were lovely. My siblings, to this day, are the best at rallying together to create comfort, fun and support whenever one of us is in need.

To be honest, I had no intention of going back to finish school or play basketball. I couldn't imagine a world where I would be brave (or stupid enough) to go back to that place. I had been miserable for months and although a big part of that was my own doing, I didn't know how to rise above.

I remember the drive back to our home in Springbank from the airport in Calgary. That long drive down Range Road 33 with the clear and monstrous Rocky Mountains on our left. It was like I had been gone for a decade. It felt so good to see the roadmarks that I had used countless times to help others find our home. The little white church at the four-way stop. The white fence that turns into a barbed-wired fence a few driveways before ours. The long row of mailboxes on the side of the road. The barn half-way down our driveway that we had converted into a basketball court. Our long green bungalow. I was home.

Magical Mentor

We have a family friend that is a few years older than me. He was in my dad's Mormon scouts group when he was a young man. He was an amazing basketball player and someone I looked up to immensely. As he grew older, my dad became his friend and mentor. Once in college, he played in the U.S. at a few different schools, always with the dream to make it to Division 1, but he never quite got there. I met up with him for a drink only a couple nights after I had gotten home.

We hung out all night, talking about everything that had happened and my resistance to go back. He was one of the few people that understood what I had been through and could truly empathize when I explained how hard the whole experience had been. After several drinks and into the early hours of the morning, we were back at his house. I had had a crush on this guy for years, and had dreamt about the opportunity to be in his arms and in his bed. Despite my obvious advances, he was a gentleman (which I appreciate now) and did not take advantage of the situation. He respected me and my family very much and, after hearing everything, he said to me: "If you don't go back, you will regret it for the rest of your life. You will always ask 'what if?'" I was not happy with this because I could feel deep down that he was right. In that moment, I knew what I had to do and it was not going to be easy.

The next day I called my coach. I apologized and told him that I wouldn't let myself quit and I want to come back. I had a flight booked a few days from then and I was ready to be all-in. He told me the team was not happy with me. I had missed a couple games, a few practices, and a few training sessions. In order for me to come back, I had to commit to making up for the missed hours along with jumping back into training and practices. I said I would do whatever it takes.

Law of Attraction

I have been lucky in my life to be surrounded by many inspiring and motivated people, more so now that I recognize the importance of these relationships. These are the people who have stood up for me, who have reassured me of my greatness over and over again and who have showed up in their own lives in such a big way that it gave me power and confidence to do the same in my life. It can be hard to decipher which voices to listen to and whose advice to take seriously when it seems like most people are quick to offer an opinion without having a full understanding of the context. My mom has commented several times on the fact that she can give me advice one day that I completely ignore but then the same advice is delivered from someone else and I will hear it, take it in, and do something with it. What is that about? I know my mom has my best interests in mind but the relationship complicates things. She will say whatever she needs to make me feel good and, as backwards as it may seem at first, that makes me not listen as intently. I want to hear from the people who are on the battlefield, who have no reason to "pump my tires," who have been through something similar and have wisdom to share from their journey.

This is why I listened and was moved to bravery by the conversation with my family friend. He had been through the process of striving for excellence in basketball. He had experienced the loss of his life-long dream of being a professional basketball player. He was down on the battlefield fighting for his goals and learning about life along the way. I trusted and admired him for this. With just one night of candid connection, he helped me see through my fear and find my courage. It was a moment of clarity.

It is important to open yourself up to the lessons and support that can only be generated through connections with others. This opens you to heartache and to tough feedback but when you find others who are mindful in their delivery and seek to guide and encourage you on your path, you can get a lot further, a lot quicker.

You may have heard the phrase "like attracts like" or "law

of attraction." These phrases speak to our nature of being attracted or repelled by the energy emitted from others. As well as the phenomenon that what you put out into the world, you will receive back. You want more love in your life? Be more loving. You want to see more patience, compassion and connection in the world? It starts with you. Your experience of the world is a reflection of your inner-state and the energy you bring into every interaction.

These are not magical ways of being that produce great things in your life as a result of a positive thought or wish. Rather, consider the fact that there is approximately 11 million bits of information being processed in your brain per second. It is not possible—or desirable—to imagine being conscious of all of that at once. We are only conscious of 15 to 50 bits of that information at any given moment (Mlodinow 2012). Everything you could possibly experience in the present moment is available to you, all 11 million bits, but your conscious thought allows you to choose what you focus on or shine your light of awareness on. Whatever you focus on, you create more of. We are creatures of habit and our neural pathways grow in strength and efficiency the more we fire energy down those connections.

I was listening to a Tony Robbins podcast[6] the other day and he shared an example of what he does with clients to help them experience the power of focus. Take 10 seconds to look around your current environment and find everything that is brown. You may be surprised to see many items in various hues of brown. Then close your eyes, and visualize your environment, and name everything that was green! Naturally, this will be quite difficult. If you are only looking for brown, you have primed yourself to cut out any information that doesn't seem applicable. This doesn't mean there isn't every other color available in your environment, you just weren't paying attention. This is how I view optimism now. I am fully aware of the brown—or the shit around me—but I am more inclined to focus on the wide array of color and beauty. Whatever you focus on, you see more of.

Now, how does law of attraction work? We are all composed

6   https://www.tonyrobbins.com/podcast/amplify-your-strengths-todd-herman/

entirely of atoms, and atoms are composed merely of energy. Atoms take in and give off light energy, and this energy is never created or destroyed, just passed along and transformed (Lipton 2013). We are all energy and this energy is contagious. You attract what you put out into the world. This does not mean you can imagine a car and manifest it into existence and into your possession. But you could manifest the energy of abundance and attract more like-minded people into your circle. From these connections and relationships of powerful like-minded people, the offers and opportunities open you up to the ability to create the life you desire. There are endless possibilities swirling around you at all times and you are not going to be receptive or aware of these unless you get out of your head and into the moment while bathing in the energy that you want more of. It is not magic: it is simply brushing the surface of what our minds are capable of.

Anabolic vs Catabolic

Recently I have come into contact with the terms "catabolic" and "anabolic" in reference to the vibration of an individual's energy. Anabolic refers to the high-vibrating and creative energy, and catabolic is the destructive and low-vibration energy. This is a simple way to perceive and feel the energy you bathe in. When in a catabolic state I feel stuck, swimming in my problems and thinking about things I cannot control or do not enjoy. There is a theme of being the victim or being in competition, a sense that everything is fought for and it is "me against YOU." In this state, I attract more of what I do not want, and my self-talk patterns have a pessimistic and "woe-is-me" tone. On the other hand, in an anabolic state, I have tapped into my unique creativity: I feel a sense of flow where the high vibration elevates me above my problems to see solutions and I am mindful of gratitude and the benefits of wherever I am in life. There is reflection, learning, and a deep understanding of the fact that imperfection and missteps can be the greatest teachers when handled with humility, pragmatism and curiosity. In this state, I attract more high-quality interactions and re-lationships (in myself and others), and my self-talk patterns reflect this in being focused on what I can control and quick to find a productive response after an impulsive reaction. It does not matter what you are experiencing—there is always a way to tune into the anabolic energy that will support you to rise above this momentary struggle to see the light. You will respond and recover with efficiency and ease when this is your practice.

At lululemon athletica, a health-conscious and leadership-focused athletic wear company I worked at for six years after University, we had similar concepts to describe the energy we bring into an interaction based on the words and tone we use. Our language to build awareness was "Above the Line" and "Below the Line."

above the line

anabolic
Possibility
creativity, flow, open, collaborative + responsive

catabolic
below the line
Fear
lack, "don't want", self-doubting, competitive + reactive

I created this image to show the many different words we can use to describe a similar concept.

It was vital for the health of the fast-paced working environment for our team to be in open and honest communication. That meant a commitment to leaving our stress at the door so we could be engaged in our personal development in a heart-centred space, while also being able to connect with and educate our customers, guests, and overall community. Being above the line is a reminder to focus on possibility and big-picture, and below the line was a place of fear and focused on what we don't want. When we perceive our energy with such awareness and intention, progress and growth becomes second-nature.

Showing up with this attitude attracts people with similar intentions into my life. These are the people that vibrate at the same frequency as I do. These are the people that hold me accountable to greatness and inspire me to work hard and smart on a daily basis. We are stronger when we surround ourselves with people that elevate us.

Motivational speaker Jim Rohn is known for highlighting the law of averages and how this relates to who we are in relationship with. He says we are each the combination of the five people we spend the most time with[7].

I often elaborate on this to explain that these people could also be authors you read or TV shows you watch. If you are watching Dr. Phil every day, I guarantee you will be influenced by his energy and vocabulary. If you go on a Jersey Shore binge, you will be affected by the energy of those relationships, issues, choices and vocabulary. It is vital to notice who you are spending energy on and whose energy you are allowing into your space on a daily basis; we are strongly influenced by our environment. It is awkward at first when you begin to detach from a friendship or relationship that no longer serves who you are or who you are becoming but soon that space will be filled with someone else's energy that can elevate and empower you to the next level of your development. At the end of the day, you have to look out for yourself and consciously choose who you allow into your energetic space. We are each responsible for our own energy, and while you can strive to elevate others by leading by example, you can't do the work for anyone but yourself.

"What you are is what you have been.
What you'll be is what you do now."

Buddha

7   Jim Rohn & Roy Smoothe, From the Album Building Your Network Marketing Business - Smoothe Mixx October 10, 2008

Your experience of the world is a reflection of your inner state and the energy you bring into every interaction.

— • —

Whatever you focus on, you create more of.

— • —

It is important to open yourself up to the lessons and support that can only be generated through connections with others. This opens you to heartache and to tough feedback but when you find others who are mindful in their delivery and seek to guide and encourage you on your path, you can get a lot further, a lot quicker.

— • —

We are all composed entirely of atoms, and atoms are composed merely of energy. Atoms take in and give off light energy, and this energy is never created or destroyed, just passed along and transformed. We are all energy and this energy is contagious. You attract what you put out into the world.

— • —

There are endless possibilities swirling around you at all times and you are not going to be receptive or aware of these unless you get out of your head and into the moment while bathing in the energy that you want more of in your life.

— • —

You are a combination of the five people you spend the most time with.

Reflect, LEARN, GROW

TRY THIS:

I call this tool the "Dope-Web." It is a list of the people, places, and pastimes, that light you up, elevate you, get you out of your head, and create the experiences and support you need to learn and grow. Something I learned from my own experiences: when I was in need of support or in need of shifting my energy in a new direction, that was the toughest state within which to come up with ideas. Who do I reach out to? What activities should I engage in? Where should I go? What reminders do I need? I would often end up sitting and stewing in negative energy because I seemed to not have the discipline or understanding of what to do instead.

The Dope-Web is your resource to look to when in need of support, and is a fun collection of ideas that will keep dopamine flowing in your system. Continue adding to the list while you are feeling good so that you can avoid the effort needed to think when you are already feeling low. Who are the people in your life that lead by example, that show up powerfully and are living a life you are inspired by? Where are the places in your home or in your city that foster high-vibration energy or shake you out of the funk of feeling isolated or stuck? Finally, what pastimes (i.e., activities) have proven to provide you a sense of flow, to inspire you or get you out of your head?

This list is an ongoing creation. Something to refer to when in need of inspiration and to add to as you discover new people, places, and pastimes that fuel you and inspire anabolic energy. Keep in mind that the goal here is not to be so structured and planned-out that you lose your ability to flow and improvise in the moment. Focus more on the energy you want to foster and spread to others. Power is in mindfulness.

1. Who are your Magical Mentors?

2. If you truly believed and were focused on the idea that "whatever we focus on we create more of," what would you consciously repeat every day until it became your autopilot?

3. Alignment in your core values is a great way to start practicing the law of attraction. If you don't know what you stand for, it is hard to attract people or opportunities that will light you up. Generally, I coach people to narrow their core values down to three to eight words (aim for five on average). Write your responses to the questions below to support your exploration of core values.

    a) What words do you STRIVE to live by? (nobody's perfect)

    b) How do you want to feel at the end of each day?

c) How do you want people to feel around you?

d) What does alignment feel like and look like in your mind and body?

e) Once you land on your core values, go through each and ask yourself:

  i) How do I define this value?

  ii) What current behaviors show that I am living this value?

  iii) What can I do to live more in alignment with these values?

CHAPTER 7: Trials and Failures

"It is by logic we prove, but by intuition we discover."

Leonardo Da Vinci

In one particularly intense practice at SDSU, I planted my foot to change directions and my foot burst through the side of my shoe. My first thought was "Oh thank God, now I can sit out of the rest of practice," but my coach yelled for me to go see our trainer and get my shoe taped back onto my foot. I completed practice and had to cut my shoe off my foot at the end. This painting was created for a fundraiser for the Student Athlete Mental Health Initiative in 2014. It represents the intensity and potential unhealthy expectations that student athletes face.

After my short stint of escaping, I came back to San Diego to find a team that had lost faith in me, coaches that didn't trust me, and a schedule that left me more exhausted than ever. To make up for the hours I missed in the gym over the week I had retreated home to Calgary, my coach set up extra training sessions with our weights and conditioning coach. I had approximately 30 hours to make up for and I was determined to pay my dues. I wanted to get back the respect I lost from my teammates and I desperately wanted to behave in ways that I could be proud of regardless of the outcome.

The first semester had not been easy for anyone. It's not supposed to be easy. But at least there was a belief that we were in it together. I broke that trust when I left and that was a lesson I will never forget. I had been so caught up in my own struggle, feeling like I had it the worst, but if I had been more open and vulnerable with my team I would have at least had a community of people that could help me feel strong. I had allowed myself to be a lone wolf in every aspect of my life there and I finally saw the strength waiting to be discovered in relationships.

The second half of the year was a blur. I was still miserable in a lot of ways but I tried to make relationships and I worked on my vulnerability. I heard the struggle of the other girls and focused on my teammates instead of wallowing in my own despair.

Last Shot

The last tournament of the season was in Denver, Colorado. If we could win the Mountain West Conference, or be one of the top three teams, we would go on to play in the big tournament that the world knows as March Madness. We were excited and hopeful, but our dreams were squashed in the quarter-finals against New Mexico.

We were down 30 points and the second line was put in to finish the game. I was excited that the season was coming to an end and surprisingly nostalgic and mindful of the fact that this was my last game as a Division 1 athlete. I knew I was going home after this and felt proud of what I overcame and worked through that year. I felt that if I could do this, I could do anything.

The clock was running out and I had the ball. I drove into the key, planted hard with my left foot, spun around to my right foot, and began to fade away for a jump shot with only a few seconds left. Just as I released the ball, the girl guarding me leaped up and swatted the ball like a volley spike out of the air to land behind my head. My eyes bulged as I heard the buzzer go. I stood there in disbelief. I thought to myself, "of course that was the last shot I'm going to carry with me for the rest of my life." A truly bizarre and traumatizing year packaged nicely into one final failed shot. I was heart-broken. I was embarrassed. I was immediately depressed and inconsolable.

Once again, I had placed my self-worth into the hands of something completely outside of my control. A lesson I clearly had to learn several times before I would understand how I was making myself the victim and creating my own demise.

The school semester ended a month later and I came home with my tail between my legs. I had been through a year that pushed me to my edge daily and that broke me several times. A year that made me question my whole life's trajectory and highlighted the fact that I was all ego and had not experienced failure in any big way before. I was shattered, lost, confused and had developed an eating disorder that was far worse than I had previously dealt with.

Mount Royal College

Within a few days of being home I was called by the coach at the University of Victoria. He had heard I was home and wanted me to come visit their campus. He said all the right things, making me wary and bringing up the pain from San Diego. I told him I wasn't ready and he continued to stay in touch and let me know how much I was wanted there. I decided to play at a local school in Calgary called Mount Royal College. I didn't know what else to do other than play basketball even though my passion for the sport was gone. The game had changed for me and, more importantly, I had changed. I began to drink and party a lot. I thought about my experience in San Diego daily and made myself feel awful for it. I would burst into tears when I tried to tell my story so I did my best to hold it in. I saw a few therapists in an attempt to work through my struggle but I quickly judged each one as incapable of helping me and continued to distance myself from the possibility of healing.

At Mount Royal it was clear that I was not the star player they hoped I would be. I had outbursts of anger and I would get lazy and defeated quickly. My energy and strength was not what it used to be and I was getting progressively worse as I continued to drink heavily and not feed my body or mind in any healthy way.

Half-way through the season, I quit; this time I did not come back. I dropped out of school and focused on partying and working (in that order).

University of Victoria

I reconnected with the UVIC coach and decided I would give this one more try. I moved to Victoria and lived in my Mormon grandparents' basement for the summer as I trained and got ready for the season. I continued to party and struggle with food but I was having fun. I am sure my reputation by this point was not flattering. It's quite surreal now to look back and see the choices I made as a result of running away from what I needed to face. My grandma could see some of these struggles and although she never brought it up in conversation, she would sometimes leave newspaper articles about the dangers of drinking and drugs cut out nicely on the dinner table for me to read in the morning.

Ritalin

I had been on several different stimulants and antidepressants for my ADHD, anxiety and depression. While this started as a healthy pursuit of finding balance, like most things in my life, I found a way to sabotage myself. The summer before heading to Victoria I was prescribed Ritalin. I loved Ritalin. When I first started this drug, I was very careful to only take it when I was supposed to and never more than what was prescribed. As I began to feel the positive effects on my mood and attention, I experimented with taking more, and more, and more. I would often take it in the evening to keep myself up all night to paint or write. This soon became another vehicle of self-harm and a scapegoat for my depression and general sadness. Things reached a tipping point when I took four times what I should take in 48 hours within an eight-hour period before a basketball practice.

Halfway through practice my heart started to race and I had my first full-blown anxiety attack. I thought I was having a heart attack and could not calm myself down. I could feel my heart pounding in every inch of my body. I was taken to the hospital in an ambulance and quickly admitted to the doctor what I had done. During the tests they took they found I had an anomaly in my heart rhythm. I was put through a series of tests over the next several months and was diagnosed with Long QT syndrome[8]. I was told that being on a stimulant long-term was going to cause further damage to my heart that was potentially irreversible. This was enough to get me off Ritalin immediately and I was grateful for the urgency of this result. I knew I was not functioning well and that I was abusing this drug, but I had a habit of self-harm and I enjoyed the energy and attention to detail that stimulants gifted me. If it weren't for that diagnosis it is very likely that I would still be on Ritalin today.

One sleepless night in Victoria I created this to represent the many layers of identity and lenses through which we perceive life (2007)

---

8   A heart rhythm condition that can potentially cause fast, chaotic heartbeats. These rapid heart-beats might trigger a sudden fainting spell, seizure or the heart stopping altogether.

By the end of that year I told myself I was done with basketball. . .again. Although it was clear that it was time to retire my sneakers, that year at UVIC was what I needed to come to the realization that I was sick and needed to say goodbye to the sport I had loved for most of my life. I didn't care about the classes I was taking; I drank, partied and made impulsive decisions in between bouts of depression. I was chronically sick with colds and flus and I cared more about getting attention from the men's basketball team than I did about winning or losing my games. And at the end of the season, I was sexually assaulted by one of the players on the men's basketball team, and yet felt that it was somehow my fault and I wasn't worth reporting the attack.

I loved my teammates and became good friends with one of the rookies in particular; we found a basement suite and moved in together for the upcoming year. I came back to Calgary for the summer to work and relax. My weekend would start on Thursday and I would party until Sunday. Generally, I would be sick and recovering Monday through Wednesday, and then do it again. I am so thankful I survived what I put my body through.

My Man

That summer I met the man of my dreams. My girlfriends had a connection to a group of boys in Edmonton. My friend Katie had dated one of these guys and, in the process of doing so, became really good friends with his friends. One of the friends was having a kegger at his parent's house on the weekend in late June. His parents were away and the plan was to take full advantage of this rare occurrence. We drove up Friday night and those of us not behind the wheel did a fair amount of pre-drinking on our way. When we arrived, we sat in the car checking out the house and out walked a striking, dark-haired, blue-eyed, muscular man. He was wearing a basketball jersey and shorts, held a beer in his hand, and walked with a confident swagger. "Who is that?" I asked with the obvious tone that I was more than interested. "That's Watt" my friend Morgan replied. "I am going to get him before the end of the weekend," I declared. My mission was set.

There was, and still is, something different about Andrew—which I eventually found out was his real name—right from the beginning of our relationship. He is confident, handsome, mysterious yet humble, and has an honest and blunt style of communication. He is not one to say anything he doesn't mean. He speaks from a deep sense of knowing who he is and what he wants, with a pure intention of being himself, unapologetically. His big blue eyes and warm smile lights me up. His infectious laugh is full of life and playfulness.

That first weekend we met was amazing. We had a fiery connection and were all over each other. The connection we had was seamless and continued to strengthen each minute we spent together.

For the rest of the summer, every weekend would bring us together. Either my crew of girls would drive up to Edmonton or Andrew and his friends would drive down to Calgary. It was easy to be with him. We both spoke our minds and tended to be sarcastic more often than not. I was the first to say "I love you." I had never said it to any man before Andrew. I said it without needing to hear it back from him. I knew he loved me, even if he didn't know it yet. I knew he was someone I wanted in my life. Every relationship I had up until that point had lasted two to four weeks. I grew tired of the company of most men and was quick to recognize when something wasn't going to work out. Generally, the end of those relationships were signalled by my realization that I would rather hang out by myself than with this other person. But with Andrew, I couldn't get enough.

Intimacy without Attachment

I went back to Victoria for school at the end of August and Andrew and I decided to try out a long-distance relationship. I was happy and excited when I was with him and completely disengaged and unhappy when we were apart. I was learning another big life lesson that would lead me to conserve a lot of energy: intimacy without attachment.

There is nourishment in things as long as you do not become

attached. Even air becomes toxic if you hold it in without the constant letting go. With "intimacy" we have a deep connection or relationship with something, yet we honor detachment by acknowledging we are full and complete as we are. We are not incomplete without whatever we are intimately connected to or striving for. It may certainly bring joy or comfort into our lives, but there are many paths to joy and comfort. I have found that when I truly embrace intimacy without attachment, I am more present and grateful for what I have and I recover quicker when I lose something I love. If your expectation is that nothing lasts forever, when something ends, it doesn't break you down as deeply or for as long as when you expect certainty and permanence. I still work hard for what I want in my life, but I am much softer in my approach and I enjoy a whole lot more in my day.

Set big goals, strive for excellence, and get excited about future plans, but let go of the idea that things must go a certain way in order for you to get the rewards or happiness that you seek.

Something that had caused so much pain and depression in my basketball career was my attachment to my identity as "Marin the star basketball player." Anytime I played poorly or lost interest in the sport, I would suddenly be left without a solid foundation for my two feet to stand on. I didn't realize the importance of loving something (or someone) while also remaining independent and content with the moment as it is. This took me years to learn and practice, and my relationship with Andrew struggled many times because of the extreme pendulum swing between total attachment and loss of myself to complete disengagement and focus on my own independence. I needed to find the balance point—intimacy without attachment.

Andrew is the only guy I had ever met that I could spend hours on end with. We were passionate and at ease around each other. Our connection continued to grow roots as we learned about each other and appreciated and loved everything the other person did. My older brother was in Edmonton learning dentistry and I was not feeling the need to stay in Victoria. What's one more transfer? I left Victoria at the end of that Fall semester and moved in with my brother in Edmonton.

Andrew and I continued our relationship and once again I found myself in a position of having everything I said I "needed" before I could be happy. I was in a wonderful relationship with an amazing guy, I was enjoying school and was deeply engaged in my philosophy classes, I still struggled with compulsive eating but had curbed a lot of that since starting this relationship, and I was living in a comfortable apartment just off campus. Yet, I still felt like something was missing and that, perhaps, something was simply wrong with me.

My "Dragon"

I was making strides forward in life yet I felt stuck in my negative thoughts and expectations of what I "should" be feeling or doing. This common and misguided idea that a certain age should look and feel a certain way is a toxic cycle to be in. As I have heard from countless yoga teachers and inspiring coaches, I was in the habit of "should-ing" all over myself. I just couldn't shake the resounding feeling of shame and self-loathing. I felt anger and disgust with myself and made it worse by sitting in judgment and shame for not being able to accept and appreciate all of the great things I had in my life. The pressure inside of me felt as though it were building and expanding without an outlet to release it. I felt like things were escalating towards an explosion.

That first summer in Edmonton was when I fell into the deep crevasse I had been flirting with for years. I was home alone in my apartment on a particularly hot day. I remember the air was dense and humid. It felt like I had nowhere to escape the uncomfortable nature of my outer or inner environment. I knew I would feel better if I went outside and got busy but I felt erratic and stuck in my own negative bubble. I was struck with a buzzing fear with no objective reason, compounded by shame for staying victim to this pessimistic mindset. It was as if my brain had ballooned up to ten times its size, in danger of bursting as I felt more vulnerable and weak with each passing moment. I ran to the kitchen and grabbed a serrated steak knife.

I started slow, watching the sharp edges rip at the skin on

my left forearm. The complete absorption into this task offered me a few moments of distraction from my otherwise frantic mind. I felt a momentary sense of relief as my skin broke and I saw small beads of blood begin to form. I finally had a visual for the pain I had been feeling inside. I knew what I was doing did not make sense, but in that moment, it seemed like my best option. I became braver and began to pull the knife as I dug it in deeper, making a long cut across my forearm. As the blood began to pour, it was like I could breathe for the first time in months. Just as quickly as the relief set it, the reality of what I had just done sunk in and the shame and anger paraded back into focus. But this time my tears felt warranted. I washed the knife and hid the evidence. I made myself a bandage as I half-heartedly cared for my self-inflicted wound.

When Andrew came over that night I made up a story to explain my injury. I pointed to the door frame where there were a few pieces of jagged wood sticking out and said I accidentally scraped my arm as I was walking in the door. He comforted me and didn't think to question me further.

Two days later, I cut myself again. It was the strangest feeling. I craved that knife on my skin. I knew that it would relieve my anxiety and unexplained anger for a few brief moments. My Elephant was on a rampage, looking for instant gratification without any foresight into the amount of shame these actions brought with them. This time my story of scraping my arm on the door did not suffice, partly because I didn't try very hard to sell the lie. Andrew looked at me with tears in his eyes, unsure of what to say or how to help me. He squeezed me tight and begged me to never do this to myself again. I cried and agreed to his pleas.

We made the trip to Calgary that next weekend and I opened up to my mom about what I had done to myself. That was the moment I decided that this person I had become was not going to continue to be a part of my story. I did not know this person. I did not like this person. I did not understand this person. My mom bandaged me up beautifully with essential oils and a wrap that hugged my arm in only the way my mom can. I felt so much love from the people around me who I had allowed into my life at this vulnerable time. It was their love and support that reassured me that I am worth loving and that I needed to start taking my mental health seriously.

I had been on this roller coaster for years and it was clear that external conditions were not going to shower me with the happy life I eagerly craved. I needed to do the work. I needed to understand my mind and body and begin taking action daily to reverse this negative cycle before it became all I would ever know. I wanted more from life. I wanted to find that little girl within me that was fearless and stood up tall in the midst of a call to adventure.

I made this as a representation of what it takes to be in a loving relationship. You must give up your heart into the hands of your partner and allow yourself to experience the highest highs and the lowest lows while trusting yourself and your partner in the safekeeping of your heart (2010)

Intuition

My struggle with fear and anxiety made me lose trust in my own mind. When people would say things like "you know what's right" or "trust your gut," I could not relate at all. I could easily persuade myself to buy into both sides of an argument and see valid pros and cons for any decision. As soon as I decided to move in one direction, I would begin to talk myself out of it and hear my own voice arguing the counter-argument. I was perpetually stuck in the middle without an opinion, without a true-north compass.

This once-opinionated and outspoken girl had become so introspective and uneasy in any decision-making process that it took a lot of time and energy simply to decide what to eat when I woke up in the morning. It was as if I needed to relearn everything I once thought I knew. This became my ultimate push to begin reading and writing about the mind in a more serious manner. I needed to get to the bottom of the "why" behind every decision I made from then on. I could no longer function on autopilot. I refused to allow myself to live in this less than desirable state any longer. It was time to get into the pilot seat and learn how to operate my machine. This experience led me to another question that I wanted to answer: "how can I tell the difference between intuition, mind-chatter, and fear?"

I found myself dropping into a pragmatic state of mind. I let go of being directed by emotions and focused solely on making decisions based on what was strategic rather than emotional or intuitive. In order to retrain my mind, I needed structure and an unwavering commitment.

There is a lot more to our actions than what appears on the surface. We are driven by our habits, experience, passion, intentions, assumptions, beliefs, and chemical makeup. I can easily confuse myself when I allow my wheels to turn, second-guessing and playing devil's advocate as I decide what actions to take and what direction to head in. I struggled for years with learning how to trust my "gut." I still need to pause and test out whether I am being driven by fear or guided by something bigger than my over-protective subconscious.

What is intuition? Do we have a connection to a higher power or higher self that offers hints, wisdom or guidance? How is this different from our mind-chatter? Which voice do we listen to?

I have played with these questions for a while now. My intuition was lost behind the loud chaos in my mind. My journey into adulthood has been a process of re-finding my voice, and learning how to harness my passion and develop self-worth, to create a direction of intention and purpose. What began as strategic goals and challenges morphed into intentional living with a flow and trust in my own inner-knowing. But how did I get to this place? What have I learned? How can you find your unique intuitive knowing rather than getting trapped in your mind-chatter?

Heuristics

I believe that a good place to start is to understand the tricks our brain can play on us. In Daniel Kahneman's book *Thinking, Fast and Slow,* he educates us on the power of heuristics. Heuristics are shortcuts, or "rules of thumb," in our mental search for understanding which influence our perception and can often be misunderstood as pure intuition. Kahneman explains that,

"the technical definition of heuristic is a simple procedure that helps find adequate, though often imperfect, answers to difficult questions. The word comes from the same root as 'eureka'."

One of the most common is the "availability heuristic" which is the reliance on information that comes to mind with ease when contemplating a topic or decision. In other words, we are biased based on what experiences we have had. You might think your intuition is guiding you to choose something, but most likely it is your subconscious that recognizes something from your past and sends you a signal that guides your impulsive decision to move forward or pull away. For example, for people who have been exposed minimally to the rainbow of skin color in the human species, when meeting someone who is a different ethnicity, their first impression and subsequent judgements will be based on what they have recently heard or experienced with someone else of that same ethnicity (or similar). This subconscious "othering" process influences what you perceive to be important information as part of your first impression.

Or, when you are deciding which politician to vote for. There is a good chance that you will vote for someone you have heard some good news about recently, rather than a result of deliberate research to create a well-thought out decision at the poll.

Reliance on information that comes to mind with ease

Although these experiences might have nothing to do with the reality of the situation at hand, it will skew your perception of what you consider to be important facts. Basically, we learn from experience, so the thoughts we come up with will be aligned with what we think we know—which is not always the same as what is "truth."

There are also "affect heuristics" which are decisions of thought and action guided by feelings of like or dislike, rather than based on thoughtful deliberation or reason. Again, this is a subconscious process, as you feel what comes up in the moment and make up a story to explain the emotion. How often have you made a decision based on a feeling of repulsion or attraction without a reasonable explanation either way? These snap decisions make perfect sense when you consider the relationship between the Elephant and Rider: our Elephant wants to feel good now and will urge you to avoid what is uncomfortable and go towards what lights you up in that moment, without any language to reason or explain this compulsion.

This is a strong urge. We don't like feeling uncomfortable or uncertain but the reality of our existence is that there is a lot of uncertainty. As soon as our happy chemicals simmer down, we are back into a state of searching for threats to our existence. Although this is not happening consciously, we feel the uneasiness that this search creates and we often look to explain it by our immediate surroundings or upcoming decisions. The result: good and bad feelings that have more to do with our overprotective and overactive system rather than the reality of our current surroundings and impending decision.

Decisions guided by feelings of like or dislike

And then there are "intuitive heuristics," which refers to our tendency to avoid difficult or complex decisions by focusing on answering an easier question instead. We can relate this back to our conversation around mental models. For example, let's suppose you are faced with the decision of whether or not to buy a house. While there are many factors to consider, you may subconsciously tap into your mental model around "success" that tells you owning a home is a top priority in order to be seen as successful. Although there are many other important factors to consider, that simple blueprint could dictate a quick decision that evokes a good feeling. It is aligned with your current mental model so it feels like the "intuitive" choice to make. In this case, we avoid the discomfort of deliberation and uncertainty by putting more weight on one small part of the equation. Not that this is a terrible way to operate, but let's at least acknowledge that being aware of this tendency will make you slow down and question your reactions rather than assume they are something they are not.

Here's another example. I have recently been in the market for a new car. Andrew knows cars much better than I do and has been doing research for weeks before we head to the dealership to test drive. Because there is a lot more I don't know when it comes to cars, I can get stuck in some minor details and use that to shift my opinion towards which car I like the most. It's a lot easier to judge a car based on color, discounts offered, or the smooth details of the interior than it is to look at the whole picture and make a critical decision with all factors considered.

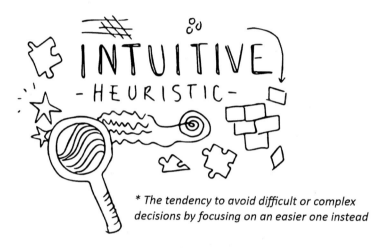

INTUITIVE
- HEURISTIC -

* The tendency to avoid difficult or complex decisions by focusing on an easier one instead

Again, these are not necessarily misguided ways to operate. On the contrary, they save us a lot of energy as they are efficient in their problem-solving skills. However, knowing that intuition is often just a short-cut decision based on imperfect reasoning from previous experience, Kahneman encourages the slower and more thoughtful route to ensure we begin to build new pathways based on what serves who we are, or who we want to be, rather than who we have accidentally become.

We are complex creatures with complex minds. What I suggest and subscribe to (which is worth repeating) is "don't believe everything you think." Acknowledge your thoughts and emotions but be wary of attaching or being swept away by seductive sensations. I view intuition as a tool for exploration and discovery. It is a whisper to dig deeper, to stay open, to dance with the moment and play with possibilities. Intuition feels like flow, rhythm and trust. It is not necessarily a magical flashlight that shines only on facts and objective truths. Intuition shines on the questions to ask and sit with; it's not just a fortune-teller. With that said, when you are able to develop a strong and collaborative relationship between your conscious (The Rider), and your subconscious (The Elephant), you are able to tap into the present moment and pick up on senses, body language, ideas, signals and patterns with much greater ease. Intuition can become something much more mystical and can connect you to a greater and higher knowing—but that takes time and practice.

I made this after a particularly stimulating philosophy class, the idea being that we are each the creators of our own reality (2008)

I believe that to tap into the fluidity and inspiration of intuition, we must acknowledge how our habits and fear try to rule us. I do not trust the first thought that comes into my mind. I play with it. I converse with it. I ask myself questions that help me understand where I have been and what I am working towards. I talk it through with people I trust. I write about it. After all of that, I am ready to have an opinion or make a big decision. But when there is no time for investigation, I let my heuristic power take the lead and I acknowledge it for what it is. In the end, I am doing the best that I can with the information I have, and while I continue to grow in many ways, I am content and grateful for who and where I am now.

When we can create a state of calm and receptiveness to our surroundings, we foster an inner environment that can calculate decisions with ease and is grounded in our direction of choice. This is why I find it so helpful to have clear goals, intentions for the day, and questions that I am curious to investigate. I view this as fuel for my intuitive and heuristic power. I know I have insight and inspiration within me and when I get out of my own way and embrace the uncertainty of life, these moments of creative genius seem to flow in with much greater consistency.

Author Elizabeth Gilbert speaks to our creative powers in her book *Big Magic* by claiming that "we are all walking repositories of buried treasure." When we can live our life driven by curiosity, rather than fear, we embody openness and discovery rather than stagnancy and resistance. Intuition is found when we let go of our need for perfection. When we let the mess of trial and error be an important part of the process, we have more energy and awareness to notice opportunities and co-create with our inner and outer environment.

~

(REPEAT AFTER ME)

With "intimacy" we have a deep connection or relationship with something, yet we honor detachment by acknowledging we are full and complete as we are.

—— • ——

Set big goals, strive for excellence, and get excited about future plans, but let go of the idea that things must go a certain way in order for you to get the rewards or happiness that you seek.

—— • ——

This common and misguided idea that a certain age should look and feel a certain way is a toxic cycle to be in.

—— • ——

Heuristics are shortcuts in our mental search for understanding and can often be misunderstood as magical intuition.

—— • ——

Knowing that intuition is often just a short-cut decision based on imperfect reasoning from experience, slow down and allow a more thoughtful route to ensure we begin to build new pathways based on what serves who we are, or who we want to be, rather than who we have accidentally become.

—— • ——

When we let the mess of trial and error be an important part of the process, we have more energy and awareness to notice opportunities.

Reflect, LEARN, GROW

TRY THIS:
    What are your "wants" in life and what are your "needs"?
Create a list for both. Acknowledge where you are spending time in
worry and trying to control something that is a "want" when you could
be nourished and balanced by spending time on your "needs."

1. What "dragons" have you fought in life? What did you learn?

2. Who have you "un-become" in order to create space for who you
truly are?

3. What is your relationship like with your intuition? What must be
consistent in your life in order to hear and understand the guidance of
your intuition?

CHAPTER 8: Death and Rebirth

"If you wish to seek peace of mind and happiness, then believe. If you wish to be a disciple of truth, then investigate."

Friedrich Nietzsche

I made this the week after Michael Jackson died. Ode to the King of Pop (2009)

Philosophy

The Fall semester of 2008 at the University of Alberta had me deeply engaged. I was excited about the approaching end of my degree, as well as my overall well-being at a place that felt more stable than it had been in many years. I had become completely enthralled by philosophy and, more specifically, the stories of each philosopher as they grappled with the big questions in life and the evolution in their own understanding. I loved the energy I would feel when I landed on a question that felt more expansive when debated and unanswered objectively. My mind would play with ideas of ways to approach the question and the many possible answers that various thinkers would come up with. I would come home from class and sit at my kitchen table for hours on end, following one thought to the next and coming up with intricate metaphors to deepen the exploration. I had stumbled into a new obsession of sorts. I connected deeply with the struggle and the passionate pursuit of questioning what had been accepted for years.

The role of the philosopher was to dissect the traditional and widely accepted views of the world to share the insight that it is much more complicated, or simple, than it may first appear. I loved that there was more emphasis on the pursuit of better questions rather than landing on the answer. I felt intoxicated with excitement as I engaged in conversations around happiness, morality, ethics, religion, feminism, and, my personal favorite, epistemology—the study of how we know things and what delineates justified belief from radical opinion. These topics of study opened my mind to the world of big thinkers and brave souls who pursued a lofty question despite the uncomfortable nature of the potential dark rabbit hole and the risk of extreme persecution.

The first philosopher that I connected with more than others, due to the similarities in our story and the questions he spent years thinking and writing about. His name was William James (1842-1910), one of the founders of Pragmatism. He was a professor at Harvard University and was considered to be the most famous psychologist and American philosopher during his lifetime. What stood out the most to me in James' work was his conflict with his deeply ingrained childhood beliefs—stemming from being raised religious—while his pragmatic and curious adult mind struggled to justify these beliefs. He seemed to never quite move past the shame and the fear of losing his religious salvation. In one of his most famous books, "The Will to Believe," he speaks to our free will to choose religion and a belief in God despite the lack of scientific evidence that your beliefs are absolute truth. One of the common threads in the philosophical work done on this subject at the time was the fear that if a society were to remove the backbone of morals and ethics that religion imposes, people would not have a blueprint to follow that would lead them to a good life. James echoed this sentiment in his reasoning for choosing to believe in God. Although science could not objectively prove God was real, the pragmatic equation discerning pros and cons led James to conclude that a belief in God outweighed the lack of belief because the moral and potential peril of our own fate was at stake.

The next philosopher to take center stage for me was German philosopher Friedrich Wilhelm Nietzsche (1844-1900), who coined the iconic phrase "that which does not kill us makes us stronger." He saw religion as having a toxic hold on humanity, offering comfort and creating mediocrity within society. He viewed religion as a numbing and avoidance tactic. In the digestible and informative BBC documentary about Nietzsche's life, "Genius of the Modern World" (2016), the host states:

"Nietzsche saw religion as a pernicious influence that encouraged an unhealthy disengagement from the world. Religion focuses on the next life, while Earth becomes a bleak exile from God. Life is seen as a thing of pain and suffering to be endured, not celebrated. This robs the here and now of sublime meaning."

The investigation of purpose, the creation of the individual moral compass, and the grappling with suffering, envy, shame and fear are all necessary in the process of overcoming your small self to find the best version of you. The rules that govern many religions teach followers to shame and avoid the very things that could teach us the most. I still remember many occasions as a young girl when I did something against the rules of the church and would feel scared for my eternal soul rather than grounded in the earthly lesson I needed to face. Of course, this is situational and not everyone will have this response. But from what I saw, heard, and learned from others, fear of sinning and shame in the repenting process was the norm.

Nietzsche often referred to the philosophical writings that attempted to simplify life into an objective concept or rule as missing the complexity of what it is to be human. Like many of the great philosophers, Nietzsche's writing tells a story as each work published showcases the growth in his thinking along with, the realizations of what a life well-lived truly is and how to achieve it. Nietzsche said, "You have your way. I have my way. As for the right way, the correct way, and the only way, it does not exist" (*Thus Spake Zarathustra*, 1883-1891).

He developed an understanding through experience that although change is hard, and transcending our individual suffering is a lot to ask, when we can rally together we can create a visceral collective experience that has the power to transform the individual. He viewed the work of the open-minded, free-spirited, and courageous creative individuals to be the curators of such change, as they unleashed their genius to elevate the world. He came to believe that we each needed to strive to be our own hero, pursuing excellence and mastery, and constructing our lives in a manner that would have us elated to be struck with the possibility of reliving our same life for eternity. In his later work, he spoke of suffering as the key ingredient to a happy life. When we overcome our obstacles and move through the resistance, this is where we create the experience of sustainable happiness.

I like to think that I can carry the torch passed on from my most influential philosophical thinkers and contemporary writers. I have often tried to simplify the purpose of life, to transform it into one objective phrase or concept, but to do so, there needs to be a foundation of context, conversation and practice, in order to land on an objective jewel of wisdom.

My deep fascination and connection to these philosophers helped me realize that my task at hand was to find my purpose in life, without the comfort and security blanket of a belief in God. What I didn't realize in that moment was that the ultimate undoing of my beliefs would require a serious earthquake within the foundation upon which I subconsciously stood for years.

I made this piece as a reminder of the importance of repetition in retraining my mind to focus on thoughts that will create the reality I desire to participate in (2015)

Existential Crisis

In one particularly fascinating philosophy class, my professor brought up the conversation of life and death. I engaged in a passionate debate with my classmates as we talked about the meaning of life, the meaning of death, and the many possibilities of both. I got home that night and sat at my kitchen table to write out a mental model of life that embodied evolution, purpose, play, growth, and had absolutely nothing to do with an almighty God. I used the allegory of an ultra-marathon and wrote feverishly about the struggles, the friends, the possible roadblocks, the resilience, the importance of breath and posture, the strength and learning from falling, the possible directions into which you can get sidetracked, the purpose of taking the journey, and the desired feelings as you crossed the finish line.

I could feel something shaking up within me. I was so intrigued and present in the existential conversation that when my brother came over I continued the discourse with him. I sat with him on the balcony as we smoked weed and talked about life and death. Marijuana continues to be a recreational and therapeutic substance in my life which generally sparks creativity or enhances the calming and grounding effects of meditation and reflection. But on this particular day, it assisted in the quick downward spiral of the rabbit hole.

As I looked up at the starry night sky, I mentioned that when I die, I am definitely coming back to haunt and play jokes on people for my own entertainment. My brother looked at me curiously. Due to the subject of our conversation and the adamant stan   had been taking on not believing in God, he said to me "that sounds kind of religious." In that moment, I was faced with my own deep-rooted cognitive dissonance. I do not believe in God, I do not believe in heaven, I do not believe in organized religion, and I do not believe in answers when the question is much more expansive and beautiful unanswered. I had been holding onto the comfort of believing there is life after death yet I also did not believe in the structure of religion that had planted that idea in my mind.

It felt like the ground had been ripped from under my feet. I suddenly felt completely unprotected and exposed for the first time in my life. There is no one watching out for me up above. If I die, that is it. There is no comfortable and imaginable world for me to land on when my earthly journey ends. It was like my eyes were finally open and I was terrified by the reality of life without assurance of safety for my eternal soul. My world began to spin and the walls of my reality began to expand far past my perception. It felt like I had been viewing life through a camera lens that had instantly shifted from being fixated on me to now seeing the bigger picture. No longer was I center of the universe but instead am now one tiny part of a much bigger, more complex system. I felt like a small bug that could be crushed at any moment. I became ill and began to cry uncontrollably.

I was not comforted by my brother's apology and back-pedalling, and I soon began to scare both him and Andrew. I ran into my room and collapsed in bed. Andrew cuddled next to me and held me as I trembled. I asked him how he has been able to function without a belief in life after death and he responded something along the lines of: "I guess I never believed anything different." Tears in his eyes, he cradled me close. It was another example of how different our upbringing and subsequent programming was. But he comforted me the way he always has. He doesn't try to fix it, he doesn't make me wrong, he just holds me, makes me feel safe, and allows me the space and time to find my way.

The next morning, I couldn't get out of bed. I was scared to leave my apartment. I felt like danger was looming all around me and I was terrified of dying. It was all I could think about, leaving me lethargic and physically sick to my stomach for three days. I called my dad, someone I knew could empathize with my situation. I explained to him through tears and gasps for air what had happened and how I was feeling. He told me he went through something similar in the three months that it took him to research his way out of the Mormon religion six years ago.

He recommended that I reach out to a group we had become acquainted with a couple of summers ago through the Institute of Religion and Science (IRAS). This group was comprised of professors, academics, passionate learners and religious advocates from around North America. I sent a heartfelt email to this group, expressing my dilemma, and requested any bits of wisdom and support they could offer.

Wisdom on Death

Here is the message I sent, which I recall writing with tears in my eyes and snorts bursting out of me. I titled the email "Life is Bittersweet":

> I have been meaning to write to you all sooner
> than now but of course procrastination is a
> powerful thing. I have however really enjoyed
> reading the discussions the rest of you have
> been having over IRASnet and I look forward to
> many more discussions to come. I am writing
> now because I had my first "real" existential

"I don't think there is any individual consciousness after death; indeed, I think it would be contra the Christian Ethic, vs the kenosis of pouring ourselves into a larger vessel. Is becoming part of gazpacho only meaningful if we get to be carrots again? We're not conscious of much of what we are, or are about, while we are ALIVE, and we continue to have effects on people that reverberate out infinitely from our lives.

Give it up babe, all you need to lose is Santa Claus.

Could we ever live as passionately, could we really ever love if we didn't really die?

It is about living, not what is before or after. Eternity is OUTSIDE TIME not before or after anything IN IT. You ever fall in love? Does it really have to last to matter? L'Chaim, girl...we've ALL been there"

John Teske

"I'm a (relatively) old-fashioned believer. I have no idea what comes after death, since in my view no revelation is around that gives sufficient detail to plan very much. (I have never felt an impulse to take harp-playing lessons, just in case that is expected in the next phase, if any, of existence.) When I asked my own father what he expected of an afterlife, his reply was always "It is my job to figure out how I can help make this world a better place during my lifetime. If God needs my help on some project in the afterlife, He'll have to ask me after I get there."

One may choose to have faith that the human enterprise (or the activity of some intelligent beings) will continue substantially beyond one's lifetime.

Your work, activities, and views may live on in this world, through genes and memes (one could expand but I think those mainly cover it.) Do what you can while alive, possibly including sharing ideas, starting programs, en-dowments, etc."

Chip Ordman

"So when I was about your age this one hit me like a brick, much as you describe, but I was blessed to have a hippie-type friend to whom I confessed my fear. He grinned and said, "Meh. Being dead is like what it was like before you were born. You've already been there." Now maybe that won't do anything for you, but for me it was transformative. I took to heart that my being is bracketed by two states of non-being, and that since I had no fear of the time before I was born, why fear the time after my life is over? The effect was to hugely magnify my grati-tude for the gift of my being-time itself, and a resolve to devote myself to its maximal actual-ization, enjoyment, productivity and service."

Ursula Goodenough

These messages helped me feel less isolated in my struggle, yet the sensation of feeling raw and cracked open, completely exposed to the world and unsafe at every turn, stayed with me day after day. The thought of death would creep into my mind and send me into a tailspin. Sometimes the thought would strike me without warning, other times I could feel the clutches of the looming darkness slowly wash over me as my thoughts followed a cycle that had become all too familiar. I would find myself consumed, scared and scratching at the walls of this deep crevasse that I just couldn't figure out how to stop falling into.

It was from that vulnerable place that I was able to rebuild the foundation of my beliefs. Each time I fell into that darkness, I would put pen to paper and begin asking and answering questions to work my way into a more present and balanced state of mind. Sometimes I would land on "what's the point?" but I was not satisfied with that and had to keep digging. I had to remind myself constantly that uncertainty in what happens after death was not the same as eternal darkness. I had to train my mind to not equate lack of knowing as the same as "nothingness." I had to accept uncertainty and allow it to be the fuel to bring me to the present moment with gratitude and excitement for the possibilities each moment offers. Each time this happened it became a little easier to get myself back up on two feet, to be able to function and connect with my surroundings. I learned to embrace that feeling and love the connection it allowed with others who were brave enough to engage in the conversation of life and death. I didn't know where I was headed, but I felt I had no choice other than to dive headfirst into this contemplation of the purpose of life and the unknown that is death.

"It's not what you don't know that gets you in trouble, it's what you know for sure that ain't so."

Mark Twain

Our ideas and beliefs continue to evolve as we learn and understand more about life and the way the world works. At one time it was not unreasonable to believe that the world was flat and was floating in space on the backs of turtles. This reminds me to stay open and allow myself to continue learning versus thinking "I know what's true." (2016)

(REPEAT AFTER ME)

The investigation of purpose, the creation of the individual moral compass, and the grappling with suffering, envy, shame and fear are all necessary in the process of overcoming your small self to find the best version of you.

——— • ———

When we overcome our obstacles, and push through the resistance, this is where we create the experience of sustainable happiness.

——— • ———

Uncertainty in what happens after death is not the same as eternal darkness.

——— • ———

Do not equate the uncertainty of death and lack of knowing as the same as "nothingness."

——— • ———

Accept uncertainty and allow it to be the fuel to bring you to the present moment with gratitude and excitement for the possibilities each moment offers.

TRY THIS:

When hit with anxiety or the feeling that all is lost or out of control, trick your mind and body into shunting off the fight or flight response by standing tall (or sit with a tall spin) with an inhale and forward fold with an exhale. Stay in this forward fold, focused on your breath, without holding any tension in your neck. Your overactive fight or flight response is signalling that you are in danger, but when you focus on your breath, fold and bow your head down, your body then gets the signal that you must not be in danger. This decreases your heart rate and cortisol stops flowing. The trick here is to engage in thoughts and actions that you would not do if you were actually in danger. For example, laugh or ask yourself deep introspective questions.

1. What do you choose to believe about death?

2. How does your perception of death affect how you show up in life?

3. What reminder do you need to tell yourself when faced with the uncertainty that death brings?

CHAPTER 9: Transformation

"Your brain responds with the strategies it has learned."

The Science of Positivity by Loretta Breuning

My recreation of Starry Starry Night (2010)

"It is always darkest before the dawn." This iconic phrase speaks volumes of truths when I look back on my life. Although I felt broken again, this was my chance to rebuild my life, my beliefs, my habits and my neural pathways, to support the person I truly was deep down. The complete loss of the foundation beneath your feet is a terrible opportunity to waste. I knew it wouldn't be easy but I also knew that I couldn't go back to the belief system I had before. The next chapter in my journey as a philosopher had begun. I had my next big question: "Is radical change truly possible and sustainable? If so, how do I make it happen?"

Relationship with Death

One thing was clear: I needed to change my relationship with death. But how? Although it is terribly painful and difficult at first, I have developed a habit of thinking about death daily. I contemplate my mortality. I express gratitude for another day of experiences and connections. I stay real with this tumultuous fact of life: death is coming for us all.

In an article written on the BBC travel website[9], writer Eric Weiner depicts his lessons learned on his recent trip to Thimphu, the capital of Bhutan. Titled "Bhutan's Dark Secret to Happiness," the article paints a picture of the Bhutan culture and their tradition of thinking about death five times a day. Known for its policy on Gross National Happiness, this society emphasizes the importance of sustainable development through non-economic aspects of well-being. To them, they have found a correlation between happiness and contemplating death. Weiner points out that, "as Buddhists say, you shouldn't fear dying any more than you fear discarding old clothes."

Other than retraining your brain to contemplate and dance with the uncertainty that arises with death, how else can we start to curb our body's overactive fight or flight response and tap into the energy of balance? It is exhausting and frustrating to feel stressed, anxious, and fearful throughout your day. We all have so much going on in our lives and at times the responsibilities on our shoulders can feel like a weight too heavy to carry. It is important to create time every day to reconnect with yourself. Slow down and connect with your breath and shine light on the benefits of wherever you are in this moment.

We have goals. We strive to be better, smarter, more successful, more experienced, more attractive, and more respected but that doesn't have to be a trade-off for joy and contentment in the moment at hand. Challenge yourself to spend ten minutes each day (I find it best to do this in the morning) to take a step back and notice how you feel and what habits you are engaging in that no longer serve who you want to be. Then get into practice. Practice being who you truly want to be. A consistent yoga practice with a teacher who reminds you of the jewel of being present will help a lot as well.

---

9   http://www.bbc.com/travel/story/20150408-bhutans-dark-secret-to-happiness, April 8, 2015

The moment you feel stress, anxiety, or fear reaching for the wheel, you can implement the techniques of mindfulness to redirect energy away from the fight or flight response and towards the problem-solving area of your brain by asking yourself quality introspective questions that ground you in the newness of this moment. The quality of your question will determine the quality of your answer and, ultimately, the quality of your mindset. Avoid bringing in judgement and unnecessary victimizing by asking "why does this always happen to me?" or "what's wrong with me?" or "why does everybody else have it easier than me?" Rather, spark curiosity and a desire to understand by asking "how do I want to show up here?" or "what do I really want out of this?" or "how do I want to feel at the end of today?" or "what reminders do I need here to ensure I lean into this struggle?"

Future Fear

Much of the fear we fall victim to can be categorized as "future fear." When we are in actual immediate danger, we react and our body does the job of getting us out of danger's way, without much thought or deliberation. The sensation of fear that is generally spoken about is the fear of potential danger in the future. Fear of death. Fear that we won't get what we want. Fear that something is lurking around the next corner. Fear that we aren't strong enough or capable enough to handle what life throws at us. Fear that life won't turn out the way we want it to.

When we talk about fear, the real question to ask is: "how do we overcome the fear of the future and go on living life in the present?"

Our fear of the future is a result of our over-protective system that either sees uncertainty and assumes the worst will happen or feels similarities to an experience that didn't go well and releases cortisol to warn you. The goal is to understand that the feeling of fear is simply energy flowing down a neural pathway, a finger pointing at what needs to be healed in your life, or a made-up prediction of what's to come that gives us a sensation of uneasiness.

For example: why do you fear making the wrong choice? You may have a limiting belief telling you that bad things happen when you make the wrong choice. This may have been true once, at one time, in one situation, but as a "rule of thumb" it does not allow for the complexity of the human condition or the importance of learning by making mistakes.

As I engaged in this conversation of life and death, I learned to approach my health differently. Working out was no longer about looking good, it was about keeping my brain and body in shape to handle life's curve balls. Although I had not had a near-death experience, this intense contemplation of death felt like an opportunity to reshape my modus operandi. Death turned into a beautiful aspect of life that allowed me to relearn how I wanted to show up and how I wanted to feel moment to moment. I don't want to be blindsided by death's grip. I don't want to be on my death bed and wonder why I didn't live more fully and enjoy life while I had the chance. I don't want to lose a loved one and then realize I never fully expressed my love or admiration for who they were. I think about death every day as a reminder that life is happening right now and I want to drink up every ounce of experience and beauty within this magical existence. And I know that movement, contentment, sweat, and challenges are actually what build resilience and keep my Elephant and Rider working harmoniously.

Motion is Lotion

While working to create these new habits and build new relationships with these complex concepts of our psyche, you have got to keep your body moving! There is something about a good sweat session that seems to make life's struggles a little more digestible. I can be in a rotten mood with a heavy heart due to various struggles in my day or life. But when I get moving, connect with my breath, and get some sweat rolling down my back, suddenly I realize I have been taking life a little too seriously. With each bead of sweat and every full belly breath, I can feel my worries melting off my shoulders.

Too much stress can begin to erode the connections you have worked hard to create and, over time, certain parts of your brain can actually begin to shrink. Luckily, we now know regeneration is a skill we can harness as we recover from life's traumas and exercise is one sure-fire way to promote that process. Exercise can cause our neurons to actually grow and create new connections that enhance our brain's functionality exponentially.

The act of getting your heart rate up and engaging with your breath in a mindful and intentional manner brings your bodily system back to equilibrium. It also releases a few growth hormones in your brain to aid in mood balancing, memory, learning, coping with future stress, and an overall sense of happiness and control. Whether you make time in the morning as part of your routine or get a sweat in at lunch or after work, it is important to make this a priority. Don't think of this just as time to work on your body but rather as a pivotal ingredient in keeping your mind healthy, stable and open.

As my yoga teacher Nora Maskey[10] says: "motion is lotion." Exercise creates the biological changes and conditions necessary for growth but what you do with that potential is up to you.

> "To keep our brains at peak performance,
> our bodies need to work hard."
>
> *Spark* by John Ratey

Birth of dope(a)me

With my ever-increasing collection of knowledge and passion for the mind-body connection, I was able to begin the process of coaching myself out of depressive states. I was making huge strides but I still felt like something was missing. In a fun-filled weekend in the summer of 2011, I finally had the paradigm shift moment I so badly craved. I branded my business—dope(a)me—from this experience (albeit three years later) as it was a vital piece to this

---

10   http://www.noramaskeyyoga.com/

ever-expanding puzzle.

I was in Vancouver visiting friends. The sun was shining and I was in the mood for a new experience and adventure. My friend had some MDMA and I was excited to let loose. For those of you who do not know, MDMA acts as a serotonin-norepinephrine-dopamine releasing agent and reuptake inhibitor. This means that not only does it release these happy chemicals that produce a feeling of euphoria, extreme empathy, connection and motivation, but it also blocks the reuptake so your system is swimming in these high-vibes. This drug is not for everyone and my intention here is to not glamorize or encourage experimentation because my anecdotal experience does not ensure yours would be the same.

I was warned that I would most likely have a rough "down period" as the drugs left my system, leaving me depleted until my body could recover from the experience. "Reality just isn't as sweet after you have experienced life on 'dizzles' (one of many slang terms for MDMA)," I was told. For me, life became sweeter.

An hour after I ingested the magic pill, I found myself walking through downtown Vancouver on my own, smiling and connecting with strangers, and dialling up one friend after another to tell them how much I loved them. I felt superb, free, detached from stress or worry, excited about whatever my future held, and so in tune with the present moment. This experience compounded into a revelation: I have felt like this before. When I eat a mindful, balanced and nourishing diet, get the sleep that I need, sweat, push outside my comfort zone, engage with inspiring and empowering people, create and actively support people around me...I feel this as a natural high.

I was sick and tired of feeling like I was missing the key ingredients to a happy life. I had been searching for passion and purpose yet I had neglected the wisdom and power that I already had within me. My MDMA experience made me realize that I am full and complete already and that, when I shift my perspective and mindset, I experience a different reality. This is the way I wanted to live my life. I had known moments with this feeling before but I wanted sustainable happiness and fewer (if any) depressive episodes. I did not want to depend on drugs, outside validation, or place my future happiness in the hands of a goal or accomplishment that would bring me only fleeting rewards. I wanted that internal, deep-rooted sense of happiness and freedom. I committed to learn and grow, and I knew that if I could live in a way that would produce this feeling of euphoria and contentment daily, I would be on the right track.

That pivotal moment sparked a curiosity to understand these happy chemicals and what it takes to create a natural high on a daily basis in a real, healthy, and sustainable way. I explored, researched, conversed with experts, and practiced with tools and ideas that I found or created. I realized that knowing about this aspect of the mind-body connection could open my mind to a new way of thinking. I began to see my emotions as by-products of my thoughts and actions. I was no longer a victim of circumstance. I began to lean into my fears and struggles as opportunities to grow and understand myself even more. I created a system that supported me to retrain my brain into healthier and more fun habits of thought and action which, consequentially, increased my overall happiness.

Knowing about these happy chemicals, how to create them, how to keep them in balance, and how to recognize when time and attention is needed to elevate them, has been life changing for me and my clients. When we actively and mindfully engage in activities that boost happy chemicals on a daily basis, consciously release stale habits with love and compassion, deliberately choose and repeat thoughts and actions that are empowering, and practice a mindset that focuses on growth and progress versus perfection and comparisons, we can increase our happiness baseline.

Happy Chemicals

"The feeling we call 'happiness' comes from four special brain chemicals: dopamine, endorphin, oxytocin, and serotonin. These 'happy chemicals' spurt when your brain sees something good for your survival. Then they turn off, so they're ready to spurt again when something good crosses your path."

Meet Your Happy Chemicals by Loretta Breuning

What are these magical happy chemicals? Where do they come from? What do you need to know about them? To be the change you want to see in yourself and in the world, you need the motivation, the tools, the path and the support. Once you are clear on your core values, your goals and the daily and incremental steps needed to align yourself with who you truly want to be, getting those happy chemicals pumping daily will make the journey so much smoother and a lot more fun. Here are the basics you need to know about your happy chemicals:

DOPAMINE

From an evolutionary perspective, as hunters and gatherers, life was strenuous and required the exertion of a lot of energy to find the basics for living. Dopamine is the happy chemical that spurts when you find something you have learned promotes your survival, and in turn, creates momentum in productivity, motivation for action, and an overall feeling of pleasure. Our deeply rooted programming rewards us with this pleasurable chemical which gives us energy to complete our task, feel a sense of accomplishment and increase our chances of going out and doing it again.

It is the feeling of a second-wind when you hear your spin motivator announce the last track of the playlist. The feeling of pride and pleasure when you pull that banana bread out of the oven. The feeling of satisfaction when you guess what your partner will say next and you are right. Or the feeling of strength and determination when someone you love is in danger and it's up to you to come to their rescue. It is the feeling of motivation when you check items off your to-do list. Dopamine feels good! You feel jazzed on life and brave in your actions. Nothing beats the motivating feeling of dopamine.

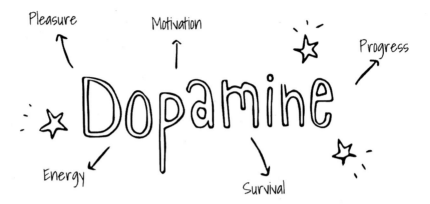

Pleasure Motivation Progress
Energy Survival

But as we know, too much of a good thing is no longer a good thing. Dopamine is a tricky chemical because, although it releases good feelings, it feels so good that we can easily fall into the trap of more, more, more. This is the chemical of addiction. We fall in love with that first high and spend the rest of our life in search of that same feeling. The problem is, our body craves novelty and you will not find that same good feeling by doing the same thing over and over.

Practice noticing your own patterns and habits. When you get attached or addicted to a sensation, it is no longer serving you—you are serving it.

Although we want to be mindful to not get addicted to our pursuit of more dopamine, there are some ways to produce this naturally and mindfully in your daily routine. Dopamine is released when you work up a sweat, set goals and take incremental steps to get there, create a to-do list and check things off as you go, practice yoga or mindful movement with intentional and focused breathing, eat a healthy and well-rounded diet including foods rich in tyrosine (i.e. bananas, avocado, almonds, green tea, chocolate, eggs, yogurt, etc.), and create a constant reason to seek as you collect experiences, resources, or knowledge. This chemical of motivation aids in sleep, memory, efficient action, mood, and overall cognitive ability and flexibility.

John Ratey tells us, in his brilliant book SPARK, that

"[dopamine] works like transmission fluid: if there's not enough... attention can't easily be shifted or can only be shifted all the way into high gear."

This makes it extremely important to find ways to elevate your dopamine levels daily and fuel the reserve tank that allows for balanced action as opposed to extreme swings from total exertion to complete lack of motivation.

SEROTONIN

Our ancestors learned quickly that we are stronger and more capable when we work together as a tribe. We adapted to strive for acknowledgement and to crave the feeling of importance, as it signaled higher chances of safety. Serotonin is the happy chemical that spurts when you do something that furthers your (real or perceived) integral role within a group. It enhances our desire for social dominance, respect, and status. It is also the reason we are in a constant state of one-upmanship and comparison. When serotonin is low, we naturally see the lives and accomplishments of others with a golden hue. We inherited a brain that seeks status and we lose serotonin and get the buzz of cortisol when we find ourselves in a low-status position, which occurs several times throughout your day (especially with the new world of social media).

Serotonin feels like safety, respect and confidence. It aids in emotional balancing, bowel regulation, and cognitive flexibility. John Ratey refers to serotonin as "the policeman of the brain because it helps keep brain activity under control. It influences mood, impulsivity, anger, and aggressiveness (2008)."

Serotonin is a powerful antidote to fear and anxiety as it targets the brainstem and amygdala directly, the areas of the brain where our programmed and habitual reactions come from.

When you are in a low serotonin state it can feel like something is wrong with the world. Your subconscious mind does not care about being rational: it views a low-status position as a survival threat.

Putting others down or being a cynic about life in general is a common reaction—and safeguard—to this feeling of low-status (Breuning 2016). You get a boost of serotonin when you nit-pick at others to momentarily make yourself feel like the better person. It can also feel good to be a cynic about life, because every time something "bad" happens, this confirms that you were "right." A met expectation, regardless of whether it is anabolic or catabolic, feels good.

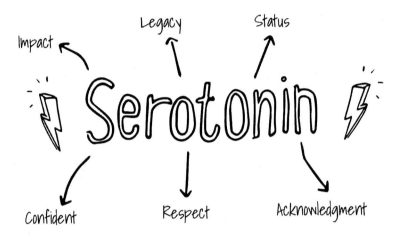

What do we do with this information? Once you can recognize these reactions and impulses as your subconscious doing its very best to promote your survival, it becomes easier to love yourself for trying and then choose a new way to respond. If your mind is seeking status, take some time to write out a gratitude journal or acknowledge yourself for what is going well in your life. Take time daily to acknowledge what you are proud of, allowing yourself to see the advantages and beauty in who and where you are now. Note that your status will naturally go up and down throughout your day, and develop the ability to notice when you feel low-status so you can practice accepting this natural ebb and flow with neutrality and openness, rather than showboating or simply posting a selfie on your social media to get your fix. This is a conversation to get into with friends, family and partners. In any healthy relationship, there is a dance and oscillation between high and low status. We all need to feel that high-status position occasionally and can find it more often when in a partnership that honours that need.

You also get some of this happy chemical when you engage in mindful movement and aerobic exercise, get sunshine and fresh air, work on a hobby or something you feel skilled at, let go of comparisons, and open yourself to new opportunities. I like to finish my day by asking and answering the question: What am I proud of? This practice of self-validation has proven to be vital.

With too much serotonin we experience lack of impulse control, depression, and seasonal affective disorder (Ratey 2008). Think of our bodies like machines. With too much or too little of the oil needed to function, problems arise.

Through this practice, we need to continue reminding ourselves to seek balance. We are not meant to feel the high-vibes of happy chemicals all day, every day. Can you breathe in contentment even when you are aware that you are currently in a low-status position? Can you breathe in gratitude even when you are not thrilled with the way your day is going? Can you breathe in trust and courage even when you feel the uncertainty and unpredictability of life all around you? Ultimately, serotonin courses through your system when you tap into your unique purpose, allowing your light to shine in this world. Carve your own path and remind yourself daily of what makes your life a gift. Serotonin will come along for the ride

.

OXYTOCIN

This is the "love chemical." We have survived and prospered because we reproduce. This chemical promotes survival with the desire for heartfelt social bonds, loving relationships, and positive interactions. From an evolutionary perspective, those who could create trusting and loving relationships had a better chance of survival as well as the opportunity to create and sustain offspring. Although we have a strong impulse for independence and a personalized experience of reality, we also recognize the need for social support and connection. We are powerful on our own but we are limitless when we come together.

Oxytocin is released when you receive or deliver tender love and care. It feels like safety, trust, love, and connection. It is an amnestic hormone which means it has the ability to wipe out previous neural pathways that lead to past lovers, as well as the ability to store faint memories of the pain of childbirth. When you reach out to give and receive support, this actually protects your cardiovascular system from the harmful effects of stress, anxiety, and fear. It works as a natural anti-inflammatory, and helps signal a state of relaxation and calm, even during stressful life events.

There are also oxytocin receptors in your heart that help heal and regenerate cells from damage. This means that even in the face of fear or the grips of stress, if we can focus on love and get some oxytocin flowing, we will recover quicker both emotionally and physically (Rankin 2015).

The iconic saying is true: "love is the answer." But of course, too much of this chemical can lead to undesirable outcomes as well. Because of its emphasis on bonds and connection, it can lead to "othering" as we are wary to connect with someone we just met or trust someone we consider to not be in our "tribe." Be mindful of the tendency of creating an "us" versus "them" mentality for no other reason than the sense of safety and belonging we get from this othering. I have found that when I focus on inclusivity as a core value, I am not sucked into the exclusive impulse this "othering" can create.

You can create oxytocin naturally—although you should still be mindful of the urge to swim in this all day, every day—when you listen to soothing music, focus on love and compassion in your responses, engage in meditative breath, laugh, have sex, get a twenty second hug, connect with friends and family, or work up a sweat while laughing and connecting with those around you. These chemicals are all interconnected and somewhat complicated. If you engage in an activity expecting to get a happy chemical boost, your strategic formula might not get the same result you might have gotten in the past.

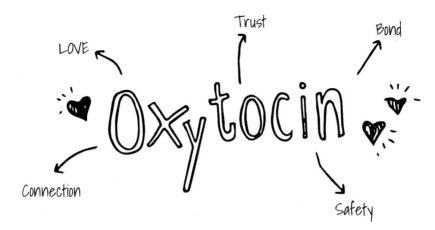

It is best to understand how to create a lifestyle that keeps these chemicals flowing but it is equally important to pay attention to what unique quantities your bodily system requires for balance, as well as the expectations you create.

Chemicals are released by our subconscious and target different areas of our body, not just our mind. As we have discussed, while we engage in self-talk in our conscious mind, this powerful chemical communication is governed by our habitual and pleasure-seeking subconscious system. While we can cognitively know that we do not want to eat five donuts, have a one-night stand, or let our partner or boss walk all over us, our subconscious wants to feel good and will keep fighting to get you to seek pleasure now. It takes time, patience and a whole lot of love to retrain our subconscious mind to see pleasure in growth, good vibes in standing up for ourselves, and comfort in self-love and healthy food choices. It simply is a matter of perspective, a shift in your expectations of your own actions, and a change in your mental model of how you view your willpower and discipline.

Again, we did not evolve to feel good all the time. It is important to note that you need to have the basic building blocks of a healthy and balanced life in order to get the full range of benefits from these chemicals. As I often state in yoga classes, we first need stability, then mobility, then look to add strength. Without the steady foundation of nourishing food, nourishing thoughts, nourishing relation-ships, hydration, sleep, sweat, and the practice of learning, we cannot generate a stable lifestyle and healthy mindset.

Know that everyone is different. What works for me is not what will necessarily work for you. As you get used to an activity that once produced a huge spurt of juicy happy chemicals, the effects begin to diminish as your mind and body craves novelty to keep these chemicals flowing. Stay open and curious to what you are feeling and allow each day to be an adventure.

We now know that our brain is flexible and resilient. Our brain is adaptable and capable of much more than we realize. The more you use it and the more you understand it, the stronger and more flexible it will be.

As you develop a new routine to actively engage in activities that produce happy chemicals, remember that the process to create new habits takes time and patience. So start practicing.

"Building new circuits in adulthood is like trying to slash a new trail through dense rainforest. Every step takes huge effort, and the new trail disappears into the undergrowth if you don't use it again soon. Such trailblazing feels inefficient and downright unsafe when a nice superhighway [i.e., habit] is nearby. That's why people tend to stick with the pathways they have."

Meet Your Happy Chemicals by Loretta Breuning, PhD

I made this for the walls at the spin studio YYC Cycle in Kensington
Calgary, Alberta (2014)

REPEAT AFTER ME

The complete loss of the foundation beneath your feet is a terrible opportunity to waste.

— • —

"You shouldn't fear dying any more than you fear discarding old clothes." — Buddhist saying

— • —

We have goals. We strive to be better, smarter, more successful, more experienced, more attractive, and more respected but that doesn't have to be a trade-off for joy and contentment in the moment at hand.

— • —

I think about death every day as a reminder that life is happening right now and I want to drink up every ounce of experience and beauty within this magical existence.

— • —

The act of getting your heart rate up and engaging with your breath in a mindful and intentional manner brings your bodily system back to equilibrium. It also releases a few growth hormones in your brain to aid in mood balancing, memory, learning, coping with future stress, and an overall sense of happiness and control.

— • —

We are powerful on our own but we are limitless when we come together.

— • —

When we actively and mindfully engage in activities that boost happy chemicals on a daily basis, consciously release stale habits with love and compassion, deliberately choose and repeat thoughts and actions that are empowering, and create a mindset that focuses on growth and progress versus perfection and comparisons, we can increase our happiness baseline.

━ • ━

Dopamine is the happy chemical that spurts when you find something you have learned promotes your survival, and in turn, creates momentum in productivity, motivation for action, and an overall feeling of pleasure.

━ • ━

When you get attached or addicted to a sensation, it no longer is serving you, rather, you are serving it.

━ • ━

Serotonin is the happy chemical that spurts when you do something that furthers your (real or perceived) integral role within a group. It enhances our desire for social dominance, respect and status.

━ • ━

Oxytocin promotes survival with the desire for heartfelt social bonds, loving relationships, and positive interactions.

━ • ━

Without the steady foundation of nourishing food, nourishing thoughts, nourishing relationships, hydration, sleep, sweat, and the practice of learning, we cannot generate a stable lifestyle and healthy mindset.

1. What do you really want out of life?

2. How do you need to show up each day to create momentum towards what you really want?

3. What does your ideal morning routine look like to tap into your ideal state of mind?

4. What are key reminders for you to ensure you are actively engaging in activities and thoughts that produce happy chemicals?

CHAPTER 10: The Road Back

"Don't ask yourself what the world needs.
Ask yourself what makes you come alive. And then go do it.
Because what the world needs is people who have come alive."

Howard Thurman

As my mood and mindset began to elevate out of darkness more consistently, my artwork took on a lighter and more playful tone. This piece represents the diversity, progression and phases of life (2014)

I graduated with a degree in philosophy in 2010 and began working at lululemon athletica a few weeks later. I changed my mind several times in regards to what I wanted to pursue as a career. I had written the LSAT and when I got my score back to see that I had a competitive chance of getting into a decent law school, I decided that that was not the avenue I wanted to head down. Of course, this decision was not made without several days and nights of ruminating and getting stuck in the rabbit hole of "what if I make the wrong choice?"

Working at lululemon seemed like a good idea for the time being. The culture, the clothes, the people, the energy, and the community it brought into my life was a gift. Although I grew tired of the retail side of the business, I was in love with everything else this culture offered. I gained more fuel for my self-study as I had daily experiences to practice what I had learned and I continued to read and explore the works of many great leaders and thinkers in my free time.

My first attempt at group facilitation was at the Kingsway Mall (Edmonton) lululemon location only a few months into my employment. There was a struggle between the management team and the educators (i.e., sales staff). The managers were getting a sense of retaliation and negative attitudes from their staff while the staff was feeling micromanaged and belittled. It was unclear where this had started but it was steadily getting worse as days went on. I had noticed this power struggle for a couple weeks and offered to lead a session in our next staff meeting to address the issue. I had recently discovered the Results Cycle in *The Heart of Coaching (2007)* by Thomas Crane during the copious amounts of reading I was doing on my own time.

Results Cycle

To summarize briefly, the Results Cycle is a cyclical diagram that shows how our beliefs are at the root of everything from how we feel, think, and behave, to the results we get, which then reinforce our beliefs. If you want to see change in the results you are getting, it starts with your beliefs. This cycle directs us towards noticing the mental models we use to operate in the world, and shines light on our self-efficacy to change the beliefs that steer us away from growth.

I found this concept to be fascinating for many reasons and since then I have adapted and added depth to this cycle so that I can use it in a powerful way with clients. I prepared a twenty-minute presentation for the staff meeting and I remember being nervous but excited by the possibility of creating change within our damaged system. I remember standing up in front of our staff of thirty people. All eyes on me. I saw smiles begin to form on their faces as I explained the paradox of the staff feeling micromanaged and untrusted and how those feelings reinforce the behaviour that is causing management to micromanage. I guided everyone into understanding the issues behind the issues and from there we could commit to starting fresh with an action plan to rebuild the relationships that had become toxic. The applause and hugs that I received after this short facilitation filled me with a sense of accomplishment and a fire was lit in my heart. I had found a service that I could provide that felt like my calling.

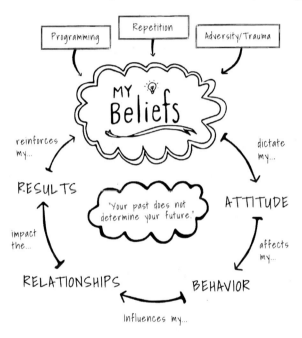

* Cycle adapted from Thomas Crane's work

This is the Results Cycle I use with clients, adapted from Thomas Crane's work and expanded from my own experience. There are three basic ways we create beliefs:

1. Programming from DNA and from what we hear or are exposed to as a child.

2. Trauma or adversity creates strong neural pathways instantly, which builds beliefs regarding what is safe and what is to be avoided.

3. Repetition—we can choose what we believe and repeat it until it be comes autopilot. We see what we believe.

After my experience facilitating at my lululemon staff meeting, I continued to look for creative ways to practice this skill and explore different ways to support the team and the individuals within it. I developed my ability to perform goal coaching sessions and was lucky to have access and support in facilitating over 100 sessions—in groups and with individuals—during my time with this company. After a couple of years, I began to reach out to small businesses, sports teams, book clubs, and friends to offer my services to anyone who was curious about bringing me in. I learned so much simply by being excited by the process of learning and growing through experience.

I stayed with lululemon for almost six years. The support system and personal development was invaluable. I learned what it meant to live with integrity grounded in my core values, how to create and host events, how to engage in and mediate difficult conversations, how to create and sustain a culture, how to create development plans and succession planning, how to enroll a group of people into an idea, how to connect with a different stranger every minute, and how to give and receive feedback with grace and love.

Limiting Beliefs

Since then, I have spent countless hours reading and exploring the Results Cycle and a few other similar models that approach limiting beliefs from different angles. More specifically, I have learned how to identify and let go of limiting beliefs and create new and empowering beliefs in their place. This is the ability to notice where there is stagnation or lack of balance, and retrain my thoughts to believe in myself and make the hard changes needed for growth and happiness. We are creatures of habit. Change can be hard. But when you have the tools and the awareness to strap on your tool belt when you need it most, change isn't so daunting anymore.

Tony Robbins refers to our young programming as our "blueprint" for life[11]. Your blueprint is the built-in triggers, assumptions, guidelines, and rules that create the lens you perceive life

---

11 https://www.youtube.com/watch?v=1iAVaUNTX9U

through. When you think about it, your limited life experience is one tiny possibility within the plethora of possible experiences and outcomes that could have happened. We are each a unique suppository of beliefs, ideas, experiences, traumas, relationships and DNA, which creates a unique perspective of life viewed through our own lens. Of course, some things in life appear to be objective and have been scientifically proven. For example: the world is round, gravity pulls us towards the Earth's core, our body has natural healing abilities when in a state of calm, our biology urges us to procreate, to live in tribes, and to move and connect. But what about the subjective beliefs and ideas that are too often taken as "facts"? Is there a right or wrong way to live? Is there a religion that is more "right" than all the others? Is there a higher purpose and meaning to life? What does a successful life look like? For most of us, we have a rehearsed "elevator pitch" when it comes to these questions, formed as a result of only a few conversations and a lot of repetition.

Through our own experience, our upbringing, our culture, our conversations, and our own internal guidance, we have an opinion and a belief which we stand on. You may believe there is only one person in the world that can be your true love. You may believe that success is a matter of how well-known and recognized you are in your community. You may believe that a good relationship should always be easy and comfortable. You may believe that some people are born with natural abilities or aptitude that predisposes them to be masters in their field. You may believe that parents should behave a certain way, your friends should always be there for you, and your hard work should always be acknowledged and noticed. Maybe this has been true for you. Maybe not. Maybe these beliefs inspire and motivate you to be in action. But maybe they deflate and defeat you before you even get started. If your core beliefs are not grounded in self-love and possibility, they are most likely taking the wind out of your sails. Life without purpose is a ship without sails, but a life without self-love is a sail without a ship.

We need a foundation of purpose and a connection to our core values in order to be grounded and disciplined in our actions. We need a practice of self-love and reflection, to witness our thoughts and actions and edit as we go. We need a deep understanding of what fuels and inspires us and take action daily to surround ourselves with, and ingest, this quality fuel. We can have everything in place but without self-love you might as well attach yourself to the person next to you and go about their day as if it were your own. If you do not consciously choose thoughts, beliefs, and actions that embody self-love, you won't have the positive impact you strive to create in this world.

As you now know, our brain's main job is to keep us alive. It does this by learning from experience. When we feel excluded or devalued, our body registers this as physical pain, which leaves a neural pathway that is sensitive to the potential danger of being vulnerable. I have come across so many people that have armored up their heart in an attempt to keep parts of themselves hidden in fear of potential rejection. It becomes a self-fulfilling prophecy as they pull away from others as self-protection, others pull away from them due to the lack of connection. The only way to find love and break these cycles of fear is to show up with your heart on your sleeve and allow the possibility of heartbreak to be less scary than the possibility of no intimate connections at all. You are limiting yourself more than you realize if you fall for the belief that you won't be okay if you lose someone or something close to you. It won't be easy, it certainly isn't desirable, but you will be okay. Death, loss and lack of fairness are the great injustices of life that we must that we must accept and grow through.

An interesting thing about your brain is that it does an amazing job at finding evidence for what it already believes. You may know the phrase, "I'll believe it when I see it." In reality, our brain follows the paradigm, "I'll see it when I believe it."

Think about that for a few moments. When we think we are "seeing" our surroundings, on average, we are actually only bringing in 40% of that sight from our eyes. The rest is filled in from experience and assumptions (Lipton 2013). We actually have more neural pathways leading from our brain to our eyes versus from our eyes to our brain. Our experiences are just as much influenced from the inside out as they are from the outside in.

Life does not have intrinsic meaning. We are meaning-making and story-telling machines. It is up to each one of us to discover our passions, to let go of our past or our habits that weigh us down, and to create a life of purpose by following our own mental models of what it takes to be our best-self. As Nietzsche so beautifully put it: "If you wish to seek peace of mind and happiness, then have faith. If you wish to be a disciple of truth, then investigate" (*Twilight of Idols* 1889).

One of the most foundation-shaking realizations that I had and that I have helped dozens of my clients experience is that most of the beliefs you have been living with are made up, passed down through the generations, or capture a skewed lesson from an early-life situation that doesn't mirror reality as a whole. These beliefs can be the result of a traumatic experience that caused your brain to create a superhighway that will light up to avoid similar situations in the future, leaving you hyper-sensitive, fearful, critical, or anxious when those memories are triggered. These beliefs become ingrained without taking into account that you are meant to evolve just as our culture and world is evolving. The beliefs you have ingrained in your mind are not necessarily wrong or self-destructive; the key is to step back and notice these beliefs. Question why you judge, assume, or critique people or situations the way you do. Limiting beliefs don't feel good: you'll be amazed when you start to notice how often you put yourself down or hold yourself back. Just reflect over the past 24 hours and ask yourself how often you said you are not good enough, it is not safe to open yourself up to life, or that you need "x" to be happy.

One of the limiting beliefs I had for many years was "if I choose to do nothing when there is opportunity for connection or an experience of some kind, this means something is wrong with me." This is a fascinating one to me. I would spend hours beating myself up and feeling guilty rather than enjoying the downtime or the space to rest that I had created for myself. I would turn a simple decision into a spiral downwards because I was fixated on the uncomfortable feeling of the tug-of-war inside of me that urged me to be out mingling and having fun while also deeply wanting to be introverted and rest my mind and body. I am quite social when I am with people but I also love and crave quality me-time. Rather than acknowledging I would rather hang out by myself and embrace the part of me that was feeling the need to retreat and hibernate, I made myself feel bad about it and was victim to the cyclical self-talk that I couldn't rid myself of. This pattern caused me to retreat more and to continuously close myself off from relationships. The making of my own doing.

I still notice this occasionally when I choose to have a night-in despite a warm and loving invitation from a friend to join in on some kind of festivity. I have moments—or several moments—of going down the rabbit hole of questioning why I chose to stay home when I probably would have enjoyed what was offered. This is when I notice the low vibration feeling in my body. I notice my breath has become shallow and I have moved below the line into a fear and lack-driven state. Fear of missing out is a tough urge to breathe through. When I get caught up in the energy of guilt and what-ifs, I don't have the energy I need to learn from the moment and make more mindful and open decisions in my present and future. The belief that something was wrong with me was limiting my ability to be content and mindful. It was limiting my energy reserves and sending me into a tailspin of negative energy and victimhood.

My new beliefs and subsequent thought patterns now allow me to alter the course of my precious energy. I remind myself....

I can't do all the things all the time.

— • —

It's okay to miss out on beautiful opportunities and allow space for other opportunities to flow in.

— • —

It's a gift to myself when I am able to be content with the decisions I make.

It's important to slow down and allow myself to move through the emotions that are manifesting as indecision and anxiety.

Suddenly, the weight of the world melts off my shoulders, and I am able to enjoy who and where I am now.

Another one of my reoccurring limiting beliefs was that "to be desirable to others I must have a flat belly and can't be dealing with food issues." This meant that anytime I felt bloated or was not in a great mood I would retreat and close myself off from connecting with others. This was such a devastating way to operate in the world. I never felt like I was enough and would perceive others' actions (or non-action) as acceptance or rejection of who I am.

To be human means we will experience ups and downs. It is from the periods of darkness and diving deep into my inner world that I uncover what needs to be healed. One of the biggest shifts I have made in the way I operate is that now when I wake up and feel the heavy feelings of depression in my body, I get a kick of excitement because I know I am going to learn and grow a lot today. If I shame myself and expect perfection from myself, I am not creating an environment where I can continue to grow, and I am certainly not abiding by one of my core values: to lead by example.

When I feel myself get triggered into a depressive state, I choose to embrace it with curiosity. What would I tell a client in this state? How would I treat a child who was struggling with this? I certainly would not tell them "it's not okay" or "something is wrong with you." I certainly would not make them feel bad for being in this place again when they have done so much work to rise above and learn from these states in the past. When we choose to embrace our reality with love, open arms, compassion, and listening ears, we create an environment to learn and grow. It doesn't always make the darkness disappear, but it will help you soften and accept where you are. What you resist, persists. What you love, you set free.

Perhaps you were told when you were young that you were too small, too weak, too inexperienced, or too slow to engage in something your heart desired. Perhaps you were punished for a behaviour that you didn't commit and, although you told the truth, you weren't listened to or believed. Perhaps you lost a parent or best friend and the pain taught you it is safer to keep people at a distance. Perhaps you were abused by an adult or you had high expectations of someone you looked up to and were let down in a big way. These moments are common, a normal experience of life, and can dictate the way you show up and take steps to protect yourself as you grow into adulthood. When we get curious and open ourselves up to noticing these patterns, we find our power to respond instead of continuing to react in these stale, habitual ways of being.

Naturally, some of the beliefs you have suit you just fine for now. It is the "limiting beliefs" we want to uncover first and foremost. The beliefs that keep you stagnant, fearful, closed from the world, armoured from failure or heartache, opposed to the opinions of others, or negative in your worldview or mindset. My wise and soulful friend Kalea Mullett[12], when asked what her experience with limiting beliefs has taught her, replied that these beliefs produce a feeling of isolation. They are the beliefs that make you feel alone, not good enough for what you want in life, and too much in your own head to actually engage and connect with people in an authentic and powerful way. Noticing and becoming aware of what sensations these limiting beliefs create in your body is a great way to build a signal to snap you out of the mind-chatter and into mindfulness.

I notice I am engaging with a limiting belief when my body language changes. My shoulders slump forward as if I a trying to protect my heart. My breathing becomes shallow. I go inward and lose my ability to connect and play with the people or environment around me. Once I tap back into mindfulness and tell myself what I need to hear, my shoulders pull back, I sit up tall, and I deepen my breath to feel the life force inside me rinse out my mind and body. From there,

---

12   https://www.kaleamullett.com/

I am able to breathe through the struggle and rise above the low vibration to create and stand tall in my new empowering belief. "I got this."

If there is a reaction, a habit, or a pattern in your life that is not serving you well, it's time to uncover and release the belief that is keeping you there. Discover the power of creating a new, empowering, and inspiring belief in its place. When you find yourself getting stuck in your "should haves" and your expectations, carrying this moment's disturbance into the next moment rather than learning and moving on, you have found a hardwired belief that may or may not be serving who you are. Our problems and disturbances need energy to survive and when we are feeling sorry for ourselves in any capacity we are spending energy to limit ourselves instead of tapping into the power of being limitless.

Pragmatic Optimism

I had a client recently stop me as I was explaining this process to express her concern with the idea of making up new beliefs whenever you felt the need. "Could this not become a gateway to naïve and selfish habits as you exempt yourself from responsibility or error and always tell yourself that you are amazing and everything is great?" To balance between these two extremes, I promote the practice of "pragmatic optimism" rather than "naïve optimism."

The naïve optimist is a person who stays happy, blissful, jolly, hopeful, or love-struck despite overwhelming evidence that something other than pure joy is appropriate at that time. The naïve optimist avoids pain and struggle, and chooses to keep smiling in spite of the natural ebb and flow of emotions. The naïve optimist chooses comfort, low-risk and easy paths, or jumps into risk blindly with the belief that everything will be just fine. You may have experienced such a person before; gleefully happy and full of energy for no apparent reason. They often resist uncomfortable conversations by referring to the "silver lining" or changing the subject rather than holding space for someone who needs to move through darker emotions. It comes across as inauthentic and it makes it difficult to truly connect. This is actually merely the shell of a person who is hiding their edges, their vulnerability, and, ultimately, their ability to exceed a life of mediocrity.

The pragmatic optimist, on the other hand, understands that life feels best when there is a practice of contentment and happiness while also recognizing that life does not require an avoidance or denial of the struggle. To be a pragmatist means to approach each situation by assessing the truth or validity of a theory or belief based on the efficacy, the previous success rate, and the observable practical consequences, separate from the initial emotional reaction. In other words, it is the practice of stepping outside the moment at hand to make a choice based on the bigger-picture outcome and not to be seduced by instant gratification of avoidance or pleasure-seeking impulsivity. A pragmatist feels the natural ebb and flow of emotions and chooses to respond rationally from a place of neutrality, after the initial instinctual reaction. Pragmatic optimists have a very skilled and wise Rider atop a well-trained and well-fuelled Elephant.

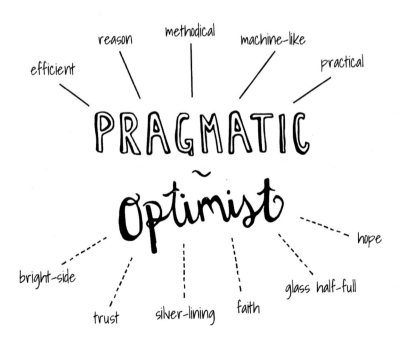

To be a pragmatic optimist is to recognize that striving for happiness, looking for the silver lining, and aligning your thoughts and actions to serve you and the world in the best way possible are ideals worth the pursuit and practice. Still, it doesn't preclude you from feeling the depths of your struggle, the breakdown of a heart broken, or the pain and suffering in the world. In my view, a pragmatic optimist follows the wisdom of Friedrich Nietzsche, who stated that suffering was not something to be redeemed from, or avoided, but to be embraced, and mastered (Reginster 2006). We must risk suffering and overcome it. Suffering can be seen as the key to finding sustainable happiness.

It is our self-discipline and our ability to flow, swim, and breathe through our struggles that creates resilience, contentment and gratitude. As Nietzsche said, "what doesn't kill you, makes you stronger."

I have lived as a pessimist, as a naïve optimist, and solely as a pragmatist. I cannot regret or shame myself for these stages of development because these lived experiences have brought me to where I am today. I know from experience that when I am committed to growth and learning, when I engage in activities that purposefully bring me joy, connection and satisfaction, and when I focus on gratitude while exploring the natural struggle of life, I feel content and passionate about the life I am living.

"Our belief systems affect our actions, goals, and perception. Individuals who come to believe that they can effect change are more likely to accomplish what they set out to do. Bandura calls that conviction 'self-efficacy.' People with self-efficacy set their sights higher, try harder, persevere longer, and show more resilience in the face of failure."

Creative Confidence by Tom and David Kelley

Subconscious Characters

There are several ways to coach yourself out of an outdated limiting belief into a new belief that inspires and elevates you. Other than sitting down with a coach or mentor and going through the models and cycles that walk you through your thought patterns, I have found success with three other avenues. One of these avenues is through my yoga practice. Each time I step on the mat, I open myself up to the roller coaster of my self-talk, my struggles, my comparisons, my judgements and my overall mind-body connection. My yoga mat is my platform to notice, witness, breathe, let go, be present with what is and expand my mind and body from being stuck in mind-chatter and into an elevated state of flow and collective consciousness. I often remind myself and my students that time on our mat is practice for life off the mat. Everything is connected when you allow it to be.

Another avenue that has afforded me huge strides in my awareness is my practice of reflection when I feel a disturbance weigh me down. When I notice a reaction that leaves me feeling icky, or a sensation of fear or anxiety that manifests in short breath and closed posture, I have found a trigger that has surfaced the limiting belief that "I am not okay and that is not okay." Whether I sit down and engage with the Results Cycle to notice where I am getting stuck and what assumptions I have made, or simply sit with what I notice and find my power and strength with my hand on my heart, the key is to slow down, find space and fuel in neutrality, and then redirect energy in the direction you desire to go. And when you can pinpoint the cognitive dissonance between the self-protective subconscious and the higher-self conscious, it becomes that much easier to navigate and tell yourself what you need to hear.

Through this process of inquiry, I discovered cyclical patterns in my limiting beliefs that surface as multiple personalities within the community that is me. While it is supportive and fascinating to notice and release these patterns with love, it is important to note that these parts of you are simply deeply ingrained habits that served to protect you at one point in time. They are not who you truly are, but rather layers of dust that have accumulated and hardened to feel like second skin.

Philosopher Carl Jung[13] wrote about these small selves and called them Archetypes, an idea that has been explored by many authors and philosophers since then. Caroline Myss[14] presents her understanding of archetypes in a simple format that I have learned to love. She refers to archetypes within four main categories: the Victim, the Saboteur, the Prostitute, and the Child. When we are in the state of our victim self, we are quick to blame others and we ask questions like "why me?" and "why do I never get what I want?" In this state we feel like the odds are stacked against us and the world is a popularity contest that we just can't seem to win. This is a very low vibration state and it is hard to be around someone else who is in their victim state. The Saboteur is the state in which you are driven by instant gratification and undermine your own power and capability out of fear and low self-esteem. This could look like focusing on what you don't want to happen until it becomes a self-fulfilling prophecy. Or you eat a dozen donuts after a full week of eating healthy and balanced. Or perhaps you are angered by others' success and you do what you can to sabotage someone else's happiness.

The Prostitute is a state in which you sell yourself short, or you are solely focused on your appearance or external reputation rather than honoring the importance of integrity and self-validation. In this state you might be more focused on money or acknowledgment and behave in ways counter to your core values to get the accolades or fleeting comfort you desire. You might be a performer of sorts, with a smile on your face and aiming to be a people-pleaser when that is not what is authentic to who and where you are in that moment.

The Child is the state in which you may feel incapable of independence. Perhaps you are wild and free and neglect to think about the consequences. This could manifest as shyness, irrational fears, naivety, being dependent on others and timid in making

---

13   http://www.carl-jung.net/archetypes.html
14   https://www.myss.com/

decisions, or simply feeling the need to be cared for and coddled.

All of these patterns are the product of childhood. They started as a self-protection reaction to something that happened, and in turn, they lock us in a false reality that perceives these characters as necessary parts of our being. Basically, we experienced some uncertainty and an arousal of fear, and rather than dealing with what was real, we create new problems we feel we have a better chance of controlling to cover up the root of the problem. While this may have worked to protect you at one time, it becomes limiting when we don't allow ourselves to evolve and embrace new beliefs about who we are and what we are capable of.

All of that preamble brings me to the third avenue to engage and get to know your limiting beliefs: give these "personalities" a name and get to know their qualities. It is important to note that these are not inherently negative aspects of you. On the contrary, each character does offer growth when you engage in the relationship and learn to harness and unleash your power. In a balanced state, these archetypes point you towards healing as you shed layers of subconscious control and step into the seat of the witness in your conscious and highest self state. From this place of observing your patterns and witnessing your archetypes, you can respond thoughtfully rather than simply react impulsively.

The Petty Pirate

I call my prostitute state the Petty Pirate. This character shows up when I am stuck in the urge for external validation and see my self-worth in the shape of my body or the platform I have to get others' attention. What started as a compulsion in an eating disorder has now morphed into a mindless eye rub when I feel low on the status pole.

When my thoughts spiral and I become consumed with worry about my appearance, my reputation, and the shell of who I am rather than the depth and complexity that is me, I find myself in a state of wanting to avoid my current reality and in need of a distraction to occupy my mind. My eyes become itchy and I begin to rub them without being fully aware of what I am doing. When I don't catch this behaviour early, it has led to a watery and swollen eye. Now when I notice the eye itch, it is my trigger to slow down, deepen my breath, clear my thoughts, and engage in gratitude. This tactic of compulsory action to avoid what is uncomfortable is something we all have in different forms and degrees. When you are able to get to a place where you feel the compulsion and allow it to be your opportunity to get curious and expand, you are able to embrace and love what is going on within instead of resist it.

Lazy Lucy

My victim character, I call Lazy Lucy—because alliteration is fun and easy to remember. This state rears its ugly head when I get stuck in the mindset of comparing myself negatively to others. Deep down, this character is a mask that attempts to hide my fear of pain and rejection by becoming lazy. Lazy Lucy says things like: "I don't care," "Others have it easier than me," and "I would rather be alone than be out in the cruel and unpredictable world." This can look like harsh judgement of myself as I get caught up in wondering if I am delusional to think that this life and business I have created is having a positive impact on others. This limiting way of being makes me want to stay home on the couch, hide from the world, and be small in my words. When I feel this character pop up, it often takes me a while to slow down and embrace her. I need to crack my heart open and share more of myself with my partner, with my community, in my yoga and spin classes, in a blog post, or throughout my day in the connections I make. I send love to those I momentarily thought negatively about—including myself—and I choose to embrace this hurt and scared part of me. This releases Lazy Lucy from my present thoughts and heals her a bit more each time. When I allow myself to sit and love Lazy Lucy I see that what I really need is a nap, a nourishing meal, or a reminder that I am not the centre of the universe. When I turn my attention on supporting and loving others, this victim state loses power.

One of the first characters that I discovered is my saboteur. She shows up as a scared, petty, selfish, and impulsive character that I call Winona's War. I call her Winona because of Winona Ryder's stint with shoplifting that tarnished her reputation years ago—and I was a big Winona fan. I refer to it as a war because it truly feels like me against the world and me against my true-self when I am in this state, although this character rarely shows herself anymore. In this state I feel anger towards myself and others, and pursue quick hits of adrenaline or other happy chemicals to momentarily rise above the heavy feelings of lack.

This is the limiting self who does not see abundance in the world and will take what isn't mine. She lacks trust in others, which I see as simply a reflection of my inner lack of trust. It is the self that was a bully, that shoplifted as a teenager and young adolescent and who took money from my dad's change jar like my life depended on those quarters and loonies. Again, this character lost strength as I sat with her, breathed through the compulsion, and got clear on what I am trying to avoid by getting a quick hit of adrenaline and instant gratification. From peace, curiosity and love, I released this pattern I was ashamed of for years.

Winona's War

Now when I get an impulse in the realm of Winona's War, I smile, breathe in love, remind myself that there is no reward or good-feeling waiting at the other end of that compulsion, and gently guide myself to take a nap or do some gentle yoga to rinse the stagnant energy off my body. It also helps to slow down and ask myself how I want to feel when I lay my head down at night. Any time I have acted out of compulsion and not out of integrity, my true remorse sets in once I am trying to fall asleep at the end of the day. A good sleep happens when I live in integrity and don't have heavy thoughts weighing me down. When I act out of alignment from who I truly want to be, sleep does not come easy.

And then there is my sweetie-pie childlike self that I call Petunia Patch. I felt this was a great name for my playful, attention-seeking, tenacious and warm-hearted self that I see when I look at pictures of me as a five-year-old.

Along with the fun and silly qualities, there is also a resounding sense of dependence and need for attention. This character sees a need for others to care and love me, and there is less of a connection to my higher self. Petunia Patch is the self who sneers at someone who wants to try a bite of my food or throws a tantrum when asked to share something I want all to myself. She is terrified by the thought of having children of her own and perfers to avoid commitment or responsibility. When this character pops up, I am reminded that I need to put my hand on my heart, love this scared and attention-seeking child for bringing my focus inwards, and remind myself that I am strong, capable, and will be okay no matter what. More often than not, this is also my signal that it is time to get some sleep or focus on self-care.

Petunia Patch

These are all characters born of my Elephant. They create the community that is within my own mind and body. They are the immature, scared and impatient qualities that I once knew as me and are fed strength when I have not given myself the self-care, love and nourishment that I need. As I have grown into the woman I am now, these qualities creep to the surface and feel like lack of alignment. These characters are a part of my subconscious programming that has been operating for years. The only way to bring these characters into balance and release the grip of their shadow-side qualities is to love them. When you appreciate and have compassion for their role in trying to protect you, only then can you begin to release their grip on you.

I can see these characters as huge players in my childhood in the way I lived my everyday life. Awareness is always the first step in the change process, and what better way to develop awareness than to turn it into a fun game of naming and playing with these beautiful and shadow-sides of my being? Through this awareness, we get to a place of acceptance and full-hearted love for these parts of ourselves.

When my Elephant and Rider are working together harmoniously, I tap into the state of my higher-self—or Magical Marin, sticking with my affinity for alliteration. This state arrives when I am grounded in my core values, mindful and content in the moment, open and receptive to my inner and outer environment, and excluding my powerful qualities as an inclusive leader, compassionate listener and growth minded improviser.

Magical Marin

It is the voice or feeling that washes over me when I notice the tailspin and am able to detach and expand my mindful presence. It is the confident voice that reminds me to deal with what happens when it happens and to not waste time and energy in the doom and gloom of possible future scenarios. It is me, standing in my power: connected, empathic, loving, and anchored. It is me, when I am able to be here now, to be content and grateful, a person of action, trusting my strength and ability, and letting things go with each exhale. That is the self I continue to build a stronger bond with. It is the self that helps me fall asleep when my head hits the pillow. She helps me notice my patterns and observe without judgement, which is ideal for creating change. She reminds me to show up ready to connect and play, aligned with the purpose of whatever I am doing while not taking myself too seriously. From this place, I notice my limiting beliefs when they pop up, see them for what they are, and consciously choose new thoughts to focus on and repeat.

Discovering your multiple personalities that pop up when triggered is a great way to begin to understand the programming you are dealing with. To build this awareness, you need to practice. A morning routine to clear your mind and set your intention and a nightly routine to reflect on your day and tell yourself what you need to hear to find balance and calm before bed. When I take a few minutes to sit, breathe, and ask and answer a few questions about how I showed up, where I held back, where I needed courage, and what moments I am proud of, I begin to uncover the trends in my thoughts and actions that will lead me to the conscious and wise self I want to know and feel more of.

Magical Marin

Winona's War

The Petty Pirate

Lazy Lucy

Petunia Patch

SUBCONSCIOUS
AUTO PILOT
95%

compulsions

reactive

triggers

CONSCIOUS
BEST SELF
5%
awareness
emotional intelligence
delayed gratification
chosen responses
mindfulness

Self Talk

Neurochemical
Communication
= EMOTIONS

desire for
instant
gratification

intuitive

habits

impulsive

fight or flight response
(average 50 - 300 per day)

Ultimately, all of this work is to create and conserve energy to be used in the direction of growth and balance. If awareness is the first step and we all have the ability to be aware, why is this still harder than it sounds? We assess whether to lean in or pull back five times per second. The average emotional pendulum swing is quite active. As soon as we feel safe from any physical threats in our surroundings, our brain immediately scans for social threats. And as soon as we perceive we belong and are safe from social threats, we then scan for purpose and a deeper meaning to our existence. And these needs are being scanned for simultaneously, no one being met excludes you from the ongoing scan for potential "threats". This overprotective mechanism can be exhausting if this is where you focus and attach your energy. Author Lissa Rankin says:

"[s]tudies show that most emotions last no longer than ninety seconds unless we attach stories to them. . . When you attach to the story, you suffer needlessly and the suffering can linger for years" (2016).

If you can recall these facts about the mind when the reminder is needed, you have an opportunity to detach from the distractions and confusing emotions that can arise with our subconscious characters. If you resist, judge or shame yourself, you feed your energy and attention into the chaos, which feeds that beast. Focus your energy on your breath, notice without judgement, discern and redirect your thoughts with pragmatic optimism and allow your emotions to flow through you intimately without attachment. Strive for the change you want to see in your life and allow your effort to be focused on learning and growing, as that outcome is always attainable.

Perfectly Imperfect
Often our desire to control is a deep-rooted idea that there is such a thing as perfection and that this is something worth striving for. Perfection is an illusion. It is an ideal that cannot exist. The very nature of being human requires us to learn from our mistakes and grow

through our experiences. Life is messy, inherently unfair, and unpredictable in many ways.

When I look back at my evolution to where I am now, I see extreme swings in every direction. As I stayed mindful and attentive to what I needed and how I felt, I slowly began to swing less and less. I am now at a point where I know what I need to think about daily to ensure I get closer to understand what my balance looks like. I notice that I feel out of balance when my breath is shallow or when my mind is running in random directions, jumping from one idea to the next or getting stuck in planning for worst-case scenarios. I notice my thoughts and actions and intentionally make adjustments when I feel myself losing my stability. The less extreme I am, the more grounded and playful I feel. It is the difference between standing on one foot swinging side to side, always trying to stay balanced, as opposed to standing solidly on both feet and generating movement with ease. There is less energy being wasted catching myself and more energy available to build flexibility and strength. And I try to remember that we are not meant to feel good all the time; I do my best to stop resisting and fighting this natural flow and save my energy for what I can control: my response after my reaction.

We are creatures of habit. You are what you repeatedly do and you will think what you have repeatedly thought in the past. Make a change today. Choose thoughts that fuel, empower, encourage, and inspire you to seek balance, to speak your truth, and to connect deeper in your relationships (including the relationship with yourself).

There is a simple and beautiful rule of life that we can count on: whatever you practice and repeat, you will improve at. And there are ways to be more efficient and intentional in your practice. When you are mindful and open to learn new ways to approach how you practice, what you practice, and what you focus on during practice, you develop the ability to get better at absolutely anything you set your mind on.

What you do daily is so much more important than what you do once in awhile. Look for a strong beginning and a strong ending, then be flexible and flow through your day. The key is commitment. The process of change is not all or nothing: an upward trajectory or an epic failure. Change comes in ebbs and flows, peaks and valleys, loops, steps backward and steps forward. Over time, it is clear that the trajectory is upwards and onward but in a small snapshot of time it can be hard to see the progress made. Commit to the process, find some joy in the journey, and know that life is that much sweeter when we are working towards goals that light us up. You are in the driver's seat of your own life, so get moving.

(2014)

"We cannot solve our problems with the same thinking
used when we created them."

Albert Einstein

(REPEAT AFTER ME)

Our beliefs are at the root of everything from how we feel, think and behave, to the results we get, which then reinforce our beliefs. If you want to see change in the results you are getting,
it starts with your beliefs.

—— • ——

If your core beliefs are not grounded in self-love and possibility, they are most likely taking the wind out of your sails. Life without purpose is a ship without sails, but a life without self-love is a sail without a ship.

—— • ——

We need a foundation of purpose and a connection to our core values in order to be grounded and disciplined in our actions.

—— • ——

Life does not have intrinsic meaning. We are meaning-making and story-telling machines. It is up to each one of us to discover our passions, to let go of our past or our habits that weigh us down, and to create a life of purpose by following our own mental models of what it takes to be our best-self.

—— • ——

To be a pragmatic optimist is to recognize that striving for happiness, looking for the silver-lining, and aligning your thoughts and actions to serve you and the world in the best way possible are ideals worth pursuing.

—— • ——

Strive for the change you want to see in your life and allow your effort to be focused on learning and growing, as that outcome is always attainable.

———— • ————

What you do daily is so much more important than what you do once in awhile.

Reflect, LEARN, GROW

TRY THIS:

Next time you get stuck in a cycle of negative thoughts or notice you are ruminating in something that does not feel good, remind yourself to T.H.I.N.K. An acronym I often use to assist in letting go of thoughts that are not contributing to my greater good.

Is it True?
Is it Helpful?
Is it Inspiring?
Is it Necessary?
Is it Kind?

I have found this acronym to be a beautiful and accessible reminder when I need it most. Similarly, there are also Byron Katie's questions from her "Do The Work" article[15].

Is it true? Can I absolutely know that it's true? How do I react, what happens, when I believe that thought? Who would I be without that thought?

Slow down and answer these quality questions to receive the quality answers you are seeking.

---

15   http://thework.com/en

1. What beliefs do you have about life that are no longer serving who you are and what you want?

2. Where do these outdated limiting beliefs come from? Can you reflect back on your childhood to pinpoint a situation where that belief was implanted or may have been true and served you well?

3. What new beliefs do you choose to repeat and practice from this day on?

4. Without self-love we do not have a foundation to stand on. What self-love mantra will you repeat for the next 21 days?

5. To know yourself more deeply, take some time to reflect and write

about the patterns of behaviour you showcase in your life.

a) What/who are your subconscious characters?

b) What triggers them?

c) How does it feel?

d) Where do they come from?

e) What qualities stand out when you feel balanced and in alignment with your true self?

CHAPTER 11: My Treasure

"Man cannot discover new oceans unless he has the courage
to lose sight of the shore."

Andre Gide

Picturesque (2010)

Purpose

With all of this work in your back pocket, we come back to
where we started: Is there an objective truth or goal that we are all
striving for? Once we have the foundation set, is there one concept
that keeps us on track? Is it balance? Contentment? Living life with
purpose? What's the most important thing? What is my gift to the
world? What is yours?

Perhaps the wisdom we are seeking lies in the questions
themselves. Progress and change are happening at an exponential
rate. What makes sense today is not necessarily going to be accepted
as cutting-edge or relevant tomorrow.

In the fascinating book *But What if We're Wrong?* by Chuck

Klosterman, he takes us on a journey of anecdotes to summarize the impossibility of knowing what the future will deem as important and from this we must acknowledge that within our predictions we need the assumption that we are wrong. He notes that it is not that we are failing to make coherent and reasoned conclusions, but rather the problem arises in our lack of asking the right questions or seeing the full picture.

In order to accept our potential wrongness as an inherent part of planning for our future, what we need is a mindset that emphasizes the importance of adaptability, mindfulness and compassion as we learn by doing and embrace the ups and downs of our imperfection. What we need is to be receptive to our ever-changing environment and allow our inner evolution to be one guided by love and curiosity. What we need is the ability to find contentment in each moment because this present moment is where the magic of life awaits.

Being open and flexible to what the present offers and the future holds is clearly a valuable quality to practice. How can we build a strong foundation of meaning and purpose while entertaining the possibilities of an unpredictable future?

In his classic book, *Man's Search for Meaning*, Victor E. Frankl displays his determined spirit and resilient mind while enduring the brutality of the Holocaust:

"[e]verything can be taken from a man but one thing: the last of the human freedoms—to choose one's attitude in any given set of circumstances, to choose one's own way. . . When we are no longer able to change a situation, we are challenged to change ourselves."

Frankl reminds us that there is a lot in life that we cannot control. Each one of us is faced with unique challenges and struggles, and when we are face-to-face with the question of "what is life's purpose?" it is up to each one of us to answer this call from within our own being. We can only respond by being fully responsible for our energy. Frankl urges us to "[l]ive as if you were living a second time, and as though you had acted wrongly the first time. . . Those who have a 'why' to live, can bear with almost any 'how'."

Whether you are seeking a deeper purpose or higher meaning to live up to or simply want to feel the rapture of being fully alive and present, it is up to you to create the life you want to live.

While it is helpful to understand the neuroscience of happiness and habits, it is not the be all end all. Meaning, joy, contentment, and purpose are fluid and cannot be boxed and contained like a formula. As soon as I think I have life figured out, my heart cracks open and I am overwhelmed with comparisons, shoulds, what-ifs, worries, and sadness. "How can I be here again?" I ask myself. "I thought I had overcome this darkness," I tell myself. But then I remember that our universe is ever-expanding and full of stark contrasts. We must dance with the balance and sometimes that means falling below our power to heal, rebuilding a stronger foundation and carving a pathway towards our higher purpose and contentment with what is.

A beautiful analogy I came across recently in an Abraham Hicks podcast[16] packages this up in a succinct way. Because we are creatures of habit, often by the time we realize we are not habitually behaving in ways that serve our higher power and higher self, it is as though we are already falling from an airplane within the path of least resistance (in our minds), plummeting towards doom and gloom. We tighten up our bootstraps, seek support, do the work, engage in the practice, consciously choose thoughts that fuel us, surround ourselves with inspiration—and we expect our life to turn around instantly. But that's not the way momentum works. You are still falling, but maybe you've been able to pull your parachute and slow the momentum. And maybe you begin to learn how to steer and develop forward momentum as you continue floating down towards the earth. It takes time and patience and whole lot of love for the journey and the process, but maybe, just maybe, you will hit the ground running.

---

16   https://www.youtube.com/watch?v=Djep-YcRT6k

Being

A warm sensation sets in when you can embrace the shadows of your being. You are not supposed to be perfect, so let go of judging yourself with that expectation. Rather than resist, what if you accepted the moment as it is and focused on breathing through the struggles? What if you allowed yourself to step outside of this moment and recall that it is always darkest before the dawn? Just as the days and years cycle, so do our own paths and inner awakening. Bring on the darkness! Remind yourself to dance your way through this and you will be stronger and more full of passion and love because of it.

In the book *Mind* by Daniel Siegal, the author explores how our health and well-being may be the result of the "linkage of differentiated parts that maximize the complexity of the system." What does this mean? Through a process of self-organization accessed through mindfulness and the pursuit of growth, we create links and integration between the many important facets of our existence and begin to piece together our unique representation of reality. The result of the quality and structural nature of those linkages will directly impact your overall well-being.

The magic of integration is the main reason I wrote this book. After years of study and practice (which are ongoing), I began to see the thread of commonality between all great self-development thinkers and systems. It was as though my view of change and development started as seemingly random dots all over a page and as I continued to explore and invest in my work, lines were drawn and images began to form, and one day a roadmap appeared.

With this in mind, I invite you to begin your integration process. We are relational and conversational beings. Without inviting this work into your current relationships, you will not see the growth you are inspired to create. This book has become my ultimate reminder and source of repetition. I have read and re-read these pages and I continue to share my experience, learnings, and curiosities with the world. I am filled with inspiration each time I do. I share my story and learnings because, as it inspires others, it also heals and empowers me each time I share it. I wrote this book for myself and when it lands in your hands and inspires you to play big and be bold, that is the icing on the cake. My goal is not to tell you how to live or to encourage you to simply follow my model of life to find and sustain happiness. I view my job as always working myself out of the job. I want you to learn how to coach, inspire, motivate, and empower yourself. While the process may begin with copying, it will evolve creatively as you discover the foundation that serves you and the capability you have to steer the wheel.

Before I guide you through the integration process, what do we need to keep in mind?

1. We are creatures of habit

We believe whatever we repeat. In other words, our subconscious does not delineate between fact and fiction, and will eat up whatever it is fed. We have created a confused system by feeding ourselves with instant gratification and have learned to avoid progress in our goals because of the initial discomfort. We have a biological craving for things that feel good now but, over time—*in excess*—can be extremely harmful (sugar, comparison, judgement, routine, sex, status, etc.). This is a part of our self-protection mechanism, as our Elephant (subconscious) mind wants to feel good now and perceives these quick-hits of pleasure as promoting survival. We want more of whatever feels good in case we do not have a chance to come across it again in the near future.

A great way to keep this in check is to remind ourselves to slow down and reconnect with our purpose and our breath. Ask yourself this question daily: "what is the most important thing to keep in mind today?" When we reflect daily on pinpointing where we are in our emotional pendulum swing, we can then assess what the day calls for in order to step back into balance. Rather than assuming life is black and white and what you need today is what you will need tomorrow and so on, choose to see yourself as an ever-expanding individual dancing on the balance point between effort and surrender.

It is time to accept that we are capable of massive amounts of cognitive growth and flexibility. Let go of expectations, comparisons, self-doubt, regret, shame, what-ifs, or any other concept that deflates you or keeps you small or stagnant. Again, I am not saying you should train yourself to never feel these emotions, rather, train yourself to see them as natural reactions and see more power and purpose in your response after the fact. Play more with self-love, acceptance, passion, surrender, gratitude, courage, intimacy without attachment, and observation without judgement. Where your mind goes, energy flows. It is time you take full responsibility for the huge compounding impact you have on yourself and the world around you.

2. "Conscious doing" becomes "subconscious being"

Even though we can know what change we want to create and what steps to take, the art of actually doing it is the hard part. While your first few attempts at positive change may feel easeful and in alignment with who you are, your autopilot then fires up and in comes resistance and struggle. Your thoughts and actions must be strategic and conscious until they can become fluid in your subconscious operating system. It starts with intentional doing: take time daily to remind yourself of why you committed to the practice you are in. Eventually, this evolves into your new way of being, where your autopilot has been retrained so that your path of least resistance now leads to the actions that serve who you are and where you want to be headed.

To create sustainable change, we need to acknowledge the relationship and role of our pleasure-seeking and habit-driven subconscious mind alongside our pragmatic and big-picture-thinking conscious mind. Change manifests with relative ease when these two systems are working together harmoniously. The ultimate goal here is to conserve and create quality positive energy to fuel the journey of your life in the direction your heart desires. If your mindset is draining your energy then you can set all the goals in the world with the very best of intentions but that won't be enough to keep you motivated and bring you peace and joy along the way. The journey is your life, not the destination. And the journey is calling your name!

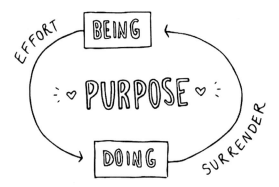

3. We need a tribe as much as we need individuality

We are programmed to be a part of a community while we strive to be unique individuals who leave a mark on the world. I believe we are meant to evolve and discover our own guidelines and motivation for action and purpose. As the saying goes: "If you stand for nothing, you will fall for anything." We have a deep-rooted program that emphasizes survival at all costs. With this survival mechanism comes the desire to grow, to create, and to leave a legacy. When we feel a deep connection and pride in our individual unique capabilities while also being connected to a community, we get to experience the strong individual within the sense of collective. Many philosophers and psychologists have written about this human condition—the search for acceptance and connection while navigating the unique experience of the individual. As you recall, we get a boost of serotonin when we feel acknowledged and respected, our bodies flow with oxytocin when we feel love, bonds and trust, and we experience the motivation of dopamine when we see that we are progressing towards a goal or taking steps that further our chances of survival. We are hardwired to crave connection and our own inner evolution.

Surround yourself with people who inspire and uplift you and honour your "me-time" to continue your path to confidence and self-empowerment. At the end of the day, it is you that needs to be proud and aligned with who you are. Individually, no one has the ability to change our world or heal what is broken, sick or lacking in our society. But if each of us honoured our own unique capabilities, and supported eachother through connection, love and creativity, I believe we would untap the genius of the collective in our generation.

4. Be open

So much of what makes us human is also what makes us a living paradox. With pleasure comes pain. With success comes tragedy. With growth comes struggle. With status comes epic failure. With life comes death. Open yourself up to the intricate and vast experience that living life to the fullest creates. Every day looks different and what you need to remind yourself of moment to moment, day to day, boils down to one goal: be open. As soon as you think you have it figured out, you close down a part of you that was ready to experience, explore and grow. When we are truly open to whatever the moment offers, we are not weighed down by expectations, we do not judge and shame ourselves, we know that context is everything and it is only our own effort that we can control. When we are open, we flow through life with purpose and a desire to connect. We remember to slow down and take in the moment as it is. We are aware and able to step back when we get signals about the need for balance. We can go all in and push ourselves outside of our comfort zone because we have the energy and the drive to play big and we trust that what doesn't kill us will make us stronger. When we are open, we face the reality of death and loss with a soft heart and a resilient soul. We mourn, we hurt, we ache, but we move and grow through these struggles because we do not avoid or resist this fact of life.

Being open is a state of expansiveness, vulnerability and strength. We acknowledge and accept our imperfect human ways and see that our perfection is found in our imperfections. We make mistakes but we put our heart and soul into our apologies and our do-overs. Being open allows us to play with life as it comes while building and creating the direction of our future.

Now that our reminders are fresh and our foundation is set, what's next? What do we focus on? What are the steps? What does it look like to get our subconscious and conscious mind to work together?

First, we need to create a roadmap of sorts so our conscious mind knows where we are headed and what steps to take as we build practice into our daily routine. It is best to keep this simple and adaptive, leaving room for exploration, discovery and growth. Second, we need to be grounded in a deep sense of the purpose behind the desired change or action. This is where we get our energy and motivation for action, along with a resilient body and mind to handle the inevitable highs and lows of the learning process. Third, we need to be mindful of our environment to ensure it is conducive to the change we seek. Surround yourself with support and inspiration, edit as you go, and find your flow.

Your roadmap will evolve as you get moving and become more clear on where you're headed. That is the fun of the journey. A little bit of uncertainty is what turns an ordinary day into an adventure.

Before we dive into creating your roadmap, which will begin in the *Reflect, Learn, Grow* section, I would like to share how I have changed my mental model around goal setting. Your happiness is not waiting at a future destination. It is what we do daily, where our mind focuses, and how we respond that matters most. To increase your happiness baseline, I propose you adopt a Goal-Setter Mindset. Setting goals is important; we know our conscious mind needs clear direction so it can guide the subconscious. But once your goals are set, turn your attention to what you do each day to develop your mental complexity and adjust your aim as you learn and figure out what's working and what's not. The Goal-Setter Mindset supports your ability to feel progress and purpose daily while you embrace the space between where you are now and where you desire to be.

As I put together my current five key steps to sustainable change and happiness, or the Goal-Setter Mindset, I noted how, six months ago, my steps looked slightly different. And I am aware that when I go through this process six months from now, again my wording will most likely change. It is important to allow ourselves to be inspired and guided by others but it is even more important to learn to be our own inner-motivator. My five key steps may serve you well and you may be able to adjust, tweak, and allow them to evolve to create a list more on par with who you are now and where you are headed.

Goal-Setter Mindset

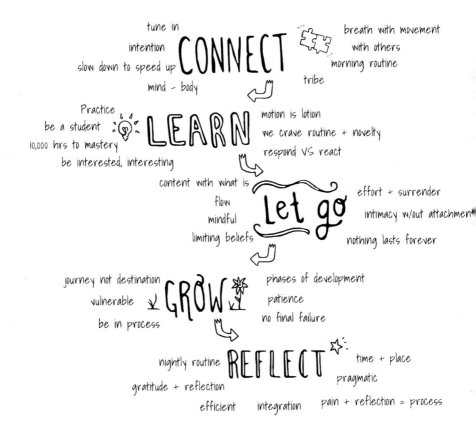

STEP 1 : CONNECT

Take time each morning to connect with yourself. Let this be a new experience, focused on being present and mindful rather than just going through the motions of a routine. Connect with your breath, tell yourself what you need to hear, and set an intention based on what you need to keep in mind to honor your growth and your balance. Connect your breath with movement. Set the stage for your day by moving your body in ways that feels nourishing and energizing. Set yourself up for success by pinpointing the action steps needed to make progress toward your goals. Choose to surround yourself and connect with inspiring people throughout your day who will support you in keeping your fire lit and your heart open. We need to lean on each other occasionally, but we also need to know it is up to us to keep ourselves motivated, on the move and in our groove.

STEP 2: LEARN

Be a student of life. Let yourself be a beginner. Enjoy the process of trying something new and being open to what you can learn from the perceptions of others. We crave routine but we also need novelty. Switch things up throughout your day to ensure you are bringing in new sensations and stimuli that will support you in your mindfulness. We learn a lot as we step back and notice our reactions and choose to respond instead of react. Be fascinated by what you notice in your patterns. Be interested, not interesting. Lastly, motion is lotion. When we sweat and move our bodies, we release growth hormones in our brain that will help us learn, adapt, and evolve into the wise and best-self creatures that we have the privilege to be. Sweat is for our brain, not just our body.

STEP 3: LET GO

What we think we own, actually owns us. Find freedom in your life by acknowledging that everything is fleeting and temporary. Enjoy the moment for what it is and then let it go. Tap into your flow throughout your day. There are activities and hobbies that you already have and love in your life that bring you into a state of flow; what are they? For me it's yoga, painting, creating, running, meditating, reading, playing, researching something that lights me up, walking and smiling at strangers, etc. There are many ways to find your flow and this is where you will fill your tank with quality fuel for your day. We can't be all effort, strategy and force. We need to let go. We need to let ourselves be and find joy in the simple things. Let go of limiting beliefs. Let go of thoughts that make you feel small, incapable, stagnant, or unworthy of what you desire. You get to choose what you focus on and what you tell yourself, so tell yourself what you need to hear and then let yourself be. We can walk around all day continuing to stack each past moment like bricks into a bag on our back. Before long, you are carrying so much weight that there is no way you can be open to the opportunities right in front of you. Uncertainty is inescapable. Failures will happen. Tragedy will strike. But so will beauty, magic, connection and brilliance. Every emotion and thought is available and waiting for you to tune in. You choose what frequency you listen to and engage in. We create more of whatever we focus on. Let go of trying to protect yourself; the more you try, the more harm you actually do. Elizabeth Gilbert, in her book *Big Magic*, reminds us, "[t]his is a world, no a womb."

STEP 4: GROW

Growth is not a straight and upward trajectory. It dips, dives, circles, ebbs and flows, which creates phases of development and stages of important stagnancy. In a snapshot of time it's easy to beat ourselves up when we perceive ourselves as taking steps backward. But really it is all forward progress as we learn and grow the most from our darkness, our missteps, and our "failures." Let yourself be in process. Let yourself be imperfect. Let yourself be vulnerable and open to your depth and you struggles. When you can learn to smile through your challenges and rise above the momentary struggles, you'll bounce back quicker and with more resilience each time. This work is not about avoiding failure, it is about learning and loving your imperfections. No failure is a final failure. It is all experience and it is all an important part of the journey. Let your cracks show and others will find the strength and courage to let their cracks show too.

> "When you give something space to be,
> you allow it to move and change."
>
> *The Gift of our Compulsions* by Mary O'Malley

STEP 5: REFLECT

There is a time and a place for reflection and it is not all day, every day. Carve out five minutes each night to reflect on your day, acknowledge where you showed strength, what you are proud of, what you are grateful for, and what you need to focus on tomorrow to keep your growth and momentum rolling. Reflect with an open heart and a pragmatic mindset. You can't change the past and it's not efficient to get caught in an emotional state as you feel your way through your learnings from your day. It is what it is. Feel it but don't soak in it. Tomorrow will be even better. Notice if you are carrying anything with you from your day. Write down what you need to remember and then let go and allow yourself to tap into self-love and balance to finish your night.

Now it's your turn to play, create and integrate. The following few pages are for you to engage in self-inquiry and develop your roapmap to coach yourself in the direction your heart desires. Use these pages to get yourself started but keep at it in your own notebook week after week.

~

YOUR ROAD MAP

Where are you now?
My core values are . . .

- How I define each one and why they matter : -

How I live these already & where I feel out of alignment . . .

Where are you headed?

In one year I will have accomplished . . .

Remember, these questions will help align your rider & elephant...

I want to feel . . .

The legacy + impact I desire to create . . .

On my death bed, I want to know . . .

I want to feel . . .

PERSONAL MISSION STATEMENT

FOR MOTIVATING YOUR ELEPHANT

The value (WHAT) you create in the world . . .

+

(WHO) you create it for . . .

+

(WHY?) What is the desired impact?

=

FOR EXAMPLE: Here is mine . . .

WHAT: Leading by example with passion, vulnerability and creativity

WHO: To inspire myself and others

WHY: To create positive change and sustain the impact we desire

Personal Mission Statement adapted from Willi...

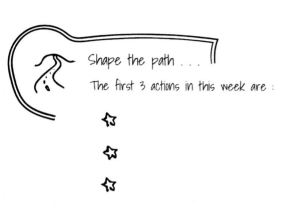

Shape the path . . .

The first 3 actions in this week are :

☆

☆

☆

What key words or phrases will be supportive reminders?

How will you hold yourself accountable?

What will bring quality fuel into your system?

What are your daily steps to the Goal Setter Mindset ?

Create a mind-map and a visual

1. What are your top ten takeaways from this book?

2. What are your five keys to happiness?

3. What are four steps to tap into your ideal "state"? Consider including these steps in your morning routine.

4. What are three mantras that drop you into a puddle of inspiring self-love?

5. What is one word to focus on this week? What does it look like, feel like, and mean to you?

6. What do you need to believe about life to create the results you desire? In other words, what are your "rules" for life? With repetition, intentional and conscious thoughts, and purposeful direction, we tap into our unique flow and rhythm of being.

7. What are you declaring as your new belief to practice and embody?

8. What rules or mantras do you need to repeat or remind yourself of daily to build momentum in a new direction?

CONCLUSION

"You think if you change things outside, you'll be okay. But nobody has ever truly become okay by changing things outside. There's always the next problem. The only real solution is to take the seat of witness consciousness and completely change your frame of reference…
No solution can possibly exist while you're lost in the
energy of a problem."

The Untethered Soul by Michael Singer

It has now been three years since I took the leap away from my career at lululemon to launch my business and become a yoga and spin instructor. There have been a lot of ups and downs but I have held strong to the belief that with practice, patience and perseverance I will carve a path that is uniquely mine and will have a positive impact on the world. After years of an intense inner-battle, I can finally say that I have found myself and I am a legitimately happy person. Don't get me wrong: I still struggle. I still have moments or days here and there where it takes a lot of energy to get myself going or to ground myself. I am not ashamed if I decide to reschedule everything planned to gift myself a full mental health day. I don't feel sorry for myself and I certainly don't get into the downward spiral by thinking I am broken, incapable or not enough. Instead, I love myself up. I put my hand on my heart and repeat "I am safe. I belong. I matter. I am perfectly imperfect." I don't resist the natural ebbs and flows of life. I let myself fall and I trust that I will bounce back stronger each time. I am able to share my story, my current struggles, and offer support from a place of desire for connection and a pursuit of instilling hope and motivation in those who feel defeated or left behind.

I truly feel like the chapter in my life that was resound-ingly saturated in darkness and pessimism is no longer a part of my being. I remember the struggle, I recall the pain and anger, and I can confidently say that my thought patterns have become aligned with who I am at my core. I am far from perfect and I make mistakes, but I love who I am and I can see that my path is unfolding in a direction that I am proud and excited about. My hope for you is that you remain curious and open to what life can teach you. Practice being conscious of your subconscious. Step into life like you are here for a reason and you don't want to hold back. You are here nonetheless, and it's worth exploring what you are truly capable of.

It's time to get out of your own way. Listen to the voices from those who are also doing their work and eagerly want to lift you up. Commit to your practice, build your roadmap and know that with time and persistence you will shed the layers and habits that don't serve you. You will grow into the sustainable, resilient, vulnerable, content, and open person you have the privilege and honour to be. Don't waste energy trying to hide. We slowly take off the armor once used to hide weaknesses, fears, and failures and dive into opportunities that could lead to heartbreak. Because what doesn't kill you makes you stronger—if you let it. Be open to discover what lights you up, what triggers your limiting beliefs, and what song your soul is dying to sing. It's time to fly.

Crossing the finish line at the 2013 Seawheeze half marathon in Vancouver, BC

"I am not what has happened to me.
I am what I choose to become."

Carl Jung

For more support and resources, head to my website.
www.dopeame.com

REFERENCES

Adele, D. (2009). The yamas & niyamas: exploring yogas ethical practice. Duluth, MN: On-Word Bound Books. (p. 22, 65, 169)

Breuning, L. G. (2017). The science of positivity: stop negative thought patterns by changing your brain chemistry. Avon, MA: Adams Media. (p. 46, 131, 137, 140, 144)

Brown, B. (2017). Rising Strong How the Ability to Reset Transforms the Way We Live, Love, Parent, and Lead. Random House Inc. (p.21)

Campbell, J. 1972. The Hero with a Thousand Faces. Princeton: Princeton University Press. (p. 18)

Catmull, E. E., & Wallace, A. (2014). Creativity, Inc.: overcoming the unseen forces that stand in the way of true inspiration. New York, NY: Random House. (p. 38)

Coates, J. (2012). The hour between dog and wolf: risk-taking, gut feelings and the biology of boom and bust. London: Fourth Estate. (p. 78)

Crane, T. The heart of coaching: Using transformational coaching to create a high-performance culture (Rev.ed). (2007). San Diego: FTA Press. (p. 150-151)

David, M. (1991). Nourishing wisdom: a mind/body approach to nutrition and well-being. New York: Bell Tower. (p. 48, 49)

Duhigg, C. 2012. The Power of Habit: Why We Do What We Do in Life and Business. New York: Random House. (p. 16)

Dweck, C. S. (2017). Mindset. London: Robinson, an imprint of Constable & Robinson Ltd. (p. 50)

Frankl, V. E. (1992). Man's search for meaning: an introduction to logo-therapy. Boston: Beacon Press. (p. 181)

Gilbert, E. (2016). Big magic: creative living beyond fear. S.l.: Riverhead Books. (p. 115)

Haidt, J. 2006. The Happiness Hypothesis. New York: Basic Books. (p. 54, 75)

Heath, Dan & Chip. (2013). Switch: How to Change Things When Change Is Hard. S.l.: Random House US. (p. 79)

Helmstetter, S. 1986. What to Say when You Talk to Yourself: The Major New Breakthrough to Managing People, Yourself, and Success. Scottsdale: Grindle Press. (p. 16, 36, 82)

James, W. (1917). The will to believe, and other essays in popular philosophy. New York: Longmans, Green and Co. (p. 119)

Kaiser, S. (2012). Find your happy: an inspirational guide to loving life to its fullest. Bloomington, IN: Balboa Press. (p. 36)

Kahneman, D. (2015). Thinking, fast and slow. New York: Farrar, Straus and Giroux. (p. 110-113)

Kelley, T., & Kelley, D. (2015). Creative confidence unleashing the creative potential within us all. New York: Harpercollins. (p. 160)

Klosterman, C. (2017). But what if we're wrong?: thinking about the present as if it were the past. New York: Blue Rider Press.g (p. 180)

Lasater, J. 2000. Living Your Yoga: Finding the Spiritual in Everyday Life. Berkeley: Rodmell Press. (p. 24)

Lipton, B. H. (2014). The honeymoon effect: the science of creating Heaven on Earth. Australia: Hay House. (p. 16, 78, 91, 154)

Millman, D. (2001). The laws of spirit: simple, powerful truths for making life work. Tiburon, CA: H.J. Kramer/New World Library. (p. 171)

Mlodinow, L. (2012). Subliminal: the revolution of the new unconscious and what it teaches us about ... (no us rights. Place of publication not identified: Allen lane., (p. 90)

Nietzsche, F. W., Soames, N., Butcher, S., Burbidge, J., Jennings, A., Cartwright, J., & Common, T. (2005). Thus spoke Zarathustra. Franklin, TN: NAXOS Audio Books Ltd. (p. 120, 161)

Nietzsche, F. W., Tille, A., Common, T., Nietzsche, F. W., Nietzsche, F. W., & Nietzsche, F. W. (1924). The case of Wagner. The twilight of the idols. Nietzsche contra Wagner. New York: Macmillan. (p. 154)

OMalley, M. (2004). The gift of our compulsions: a revolutionary approach to self-acceptance and healing. Novato: New World Library. (p. 86, 189)

Pressfield, S. (2012). The war of art: break through the blocks and win your inner creative battles. New York: Black Irish Entertainment. (p. 59, 70)

Quinn, R. E. (2004). Building the bridge as you walk on it: a guide for leading change. San Francisco: Jossey-Bass. (p. 28)

Rankin, L. 2015. The Anatomy of a Calling: A Doctor's Journey from the Head to the Heart and a Prescription for Finding Your Life's Purpose. New York: Rodale (p. 6)

Rankin, L. 2016. The Fear Cure: Cultivating Courage as Medicine for the Body, Mind, and Soul. Hay House Inc. (p. 11, 34, 142, 171)

Ratey, J. J. (1997). Shadow syndromes: recognizing and coping with the hidden psychological disorders that can .. Place of publication not identified: Diane Pub Co. (p. 78)

Ratey, J. J., & Hagerman, E. (2013). Spark: the revolutionary new science of exercise and the brain. New York: Little, Brown and Company. (p. 135, 139, 141)

Reginster, B. (2008). The affirmation of life: Nietzsche on overcoming nihilism. Cambridge, MA: Harvard University Press. (p. 160)

Robbins, T. (n.d.). The Psychology of Success [Web log post]. Retrieved from https://www.tonyrobbins.com/podcast/episode-11/ (p. 92)

Siegel, D. J. (2016). Mind: a journey to the heart of being human. New York: W W Norton & Co Inc. (p. 182, 183)

Singer, M. A. (2013). The untethered soul: the journey beyond yourself. Oakland, CA: Noetic Books, Institute of Noetic Sciences, New Harbinger Publications, Inc. (p. 34, 35, 199)

Waitzkin, J. (2008). The art of learning: a journey in the pursuit of excellence. London: Simon & Schuster. (p. 51)